Z983534

Community Learning & Libraries
Cymuned Ddysgu a Llyfrgelloedd

This item should be returned or renewed by the last date stamped below.

1 0 MAR 2020

To renew visit:

www.newport.gov.uk/libraries

D1610299

Customer Experience Branding

Driving engagement through surprise and innovation

Thomas Gad

KoganPage

Publisher's note
Every possible effort has been made to ensure that the information contained in this book is accurate at the time of going to press, and the publishers and author cannot accept responsibility for any errors or omissions, however caused. No responsibility for loss or damage occasioned to any person acting, or refraining from action, as a result of the material in this publication can be accepted by the editor, the publisher or the author.

First published in Great Britain and the United States in 2016 by Kogan Page Limited

2nd Floor, 45 Gee Street
London
EC1V 3RS
United Kingdom

1518 Walnut Street, Suite 1100
Philadelphia PA 19102
USA

4737/23 Ansari Road
Daryaganj
New Delhi 110002
India

© Thomas Gad 2016

ISBN   978 0 7494 7750 9
E-ISBN   978 0 7494 7751 6

British Library Cataloguing-in-Publication Data

A CIP record for this book is available from the British Library.

Library of Congress Control Number

2016951183

Typeset by Graphicraft Limited, Hong Kong
Print production managed by Jellyfish
Printed and bound in Great Britain by CPI Group (UK) Ltd, Croydon CR0 4YY

ABOUT THE AUTHOR

Thomas Gad is an inspirational and experienced international branding authority, with more than 30 years of experience and connections with many famous brands (including Nokia, BMW, Virgin, SAS, Deutsche Bank, Spotify and more).

His acclaimed book *4D Branding*, with a foreword by Richard Branson, was published in January 2001 by Financial Times/Prentice Hall.

Thomas Gad also co-wrote a number of books, including *Managing Brand Me* with Annette Rosencreutz (2002) about personal branding, and he contributed to *Beyond Branding* (2003) and *Brands With A Conscience* (2016), both edited by Nicholas Ind.

He is based in Stockholm, Hamburg and Palo Alto, California, and has his own international consultancy business with practices in Scandinavia, Germany, USA, Russia and the UK.

CONTENTS

FIGURES

FOREWORD

Your brand or your name is simply your reputation, you have to fight in life to protect that, as it means everything. Nothing is more important.

I think people see the Virgin brand as not taking itself too seriously; it's a fun brand, an adventurous brand, it generally offers great quality at great value. It's a people brand. Although the thought of having over 400 companies under a single brand may sound overwhelming, contrary to appearances, Virgin is focused: our customers and investors relate to us more as an idea or philosophy than as a company. We offer the Virgin experience, and make sure it is consistent across all sectors. It's all about the customer experience branding.

The most important thing about running a company is to remember at all times what a company is. A company is simply a group of people. As a leader of people, you have to be a great listener, a great motivator, very good at praising and looking for the best in people. People are no different from flowers. If you water flowers they flourish; if you praise people they flourish, and that's a critical attribute of a leader.

As a brand leader, I know that a large part of success is having a clear vision, direction and mission, and understanding the idea that doing meaningful things that your audience cares about builds the relationship between your brand and your audience.

Do you know what makes your organization different from or better than your competitors? Do you have a core mission and set company values? Do your employees describe your company culture in the same way? Do you know your audience and what is meaningful to them? If not, everyone in your organization may not be on the same page and you may not be actively building brand trust.

When Thomas Gad introduced *4-D Branding* in his book with the same title 15 years ago, I wrote the foreword because I felt branding in the 21st century required sensitivity and imagination. I still do, and one-dimensional branding has definitely given way to four-dimensional branding. Now years later, a mature online and social media dominated world with brands connecting with people everywhere requires even more of brands. Great brands that stand for something, that people believe in and that matter to them. Values and brands are inextricably linked, and to build sensitive brands with strong, persuasive and long-lasting values is far from easy.

For every branding success there are a great many failures. Relationships are not quickly or easily built. You can't fake them. Values cannot be speedily forgotten if it is inconvenient or commercially expedient. Values have to have meaning and longevity; otherwise they are valueless. You cannot embrace innovation up to a point or only sometimes. These 'relation brands' are today key to commercial success and they demand commitment – commitment to continual re-invention, striking chords with people to stir their emotions, and commitment to imagination. It is easy to be cynical about such things, much harder to be successful.

In this new book Thomas Gad focuses on the customer experience aspect and the relation brand is a part of it. One idea of this book that I really like and agree with is the importance of surprise as an element to create and maintain a great brand. I do this myself, as much as I can. As well as being fun, surprises are also a really important way to let people know how you feel about them. Little gifts and surprises are just a wonderful way of telling somebody that you love them.

In *Customer Experience Branding* Thomas Gad lays the groundwork for understanding how relation brands really do work, and presents tools for business leaders that are easily understood and effective. His message, and the growing power of branding, demands recognition, no matter what your business.

Richard Branson

PREFACE

The fact that you have chosen to read this book is, most likely, going to have an impact on your ability to embrace and benefit from the customer experience branding possibilities. The power of these insights is that strong and quick.

If you then also truly read the book and share it with your colleagues, or your top business team, the likelihood that your business will substantially benefit increases greatly.

When I wrote the book *4-D Branding: Cracking the Corporate Code of the Network Economy* in 2000, I was inspired by the changes in business that I felt were just around the corner or, in fact, had already begun. I felt that business leaders needed new strategies and models to handle the new situation. I based my approach and my branding models on my communication and marketing experience over the previous 15 years or so, including the introduction of Nokia as an international household brand.

Now, all these gut-feelings have become realities and, unfortunately, they have become even more dramatic agents of change than I, at least, could honestly anticipate. I now feel that the time is right to take a new look around the corner of what is to come. A new look based on what has already happened in the past five to 15 years. It's time to see what we can learn from some of the successful businesses and brands over these years.

I would also like to explore how branding as a concept is becoming the best tool for what business leaders believe is the most important competitive challenge for the years to come: customer experience.

It's a fact that we have already experienced the largest change in not only the history of human communication, but also in human culture globally. The internet and its mobile applications provides a greater and more dramatic empowerment of individuals that anything that has happened before. The force of this huge game-changing element is still not easy to understand or accept. Even though the impact of the internet has now matured, we simply lack the perspective needed to easily understand it. As is always the case with major changes.

We have already experienced the impact this technology has had in our lives on an individual scale, and even more so on the mega scale. Dramatic political changes in many parts of the world and a truly international financial crisis have been caused partly by a brutally integrated and transparent world economy.

Still, the most shocking difference between then and now is the new role of the individual. Instead of just being an anonymous number in the masses, the individual is now connected to other individuals on a massive scale. Thus becoming as powerful as any average individual human has ever had the possibility to become before. In this context, I always think of a quote from Anita Roddick, founder of the Body Shop and an enterpriser before her time: 'If you think you're too small to have an impact, try going to bed with a mosquito in the room'. This is more true now than ever.

I have written this book against this background. In my practice, I have met so many business leaders who have great difficulty in handling the customer experience situations in today's ultra-communication environment. When almost everybody has an internet connection and an almost unlimited, instant access to information, then the free flow of information is hard or impossible to limit or control. This creates a transparency that is almost total and that has greater impact than the media oracle Marshall McLuhan of the 1980s could ever imagine when he coined the term 'The media is the message'.

The result: if you depend on the attitude and the reactions of people, you have to take this massive human interaction between individuals into account and change your own leadership strategy – turning this threat into a possibility.

There are other aspects that have an impact in the wake of all this that requires a major change in modus operandi. Like the globalization that brings with it a 'similarization'. This makes it extremely important to try to make a difference, even if only on a small scale.

Last but not least, and for many established enterprises very important, are the challenges from the 'tiger economies' and the gradual disappearance of technical advantages and differences between the same product at different price levels.

The result: is a new approach needed to stay on top? Most likely. A new difference has to be created. A new leadership mind-set has to be established and new management systems have to be created to manage the situation long term.

There is a parallel here with sports. There is less and less tangible physical difference between athletes, in equipment, physiology and training, to differentiate between the winner and the runner-up. The mental training, the psychological preparation and the perception of how to win are becoming more import in sports than ever. This is also the case with branding – the tangible differences are smaller, or even non-existent. Branding and customer experience is becoming a mental game, much more than it used to be.

In addition to this background to the book, there is also my dedication to help enterprises of all kinds – private, governmental, commercial, cultural, industrial or even individuals – to develop new and effective strategies and instruments to handle the new situations that are driven by the impact of the network technologies.

At the end of the day, human life and culture has always been about interaction between human beings. Today, these human interactions have been scaled up with the help of technology. What you need now is to find your own business strategy that relates to your own people, your own customers or users, the public and your competitors. If you do this right, it will have a great impact on the perceived value and attraction of your offerings, whether they are products, services or ideas. If you don't do this, others will pass you by and you will eventually go out of business, or at least face serious difficulties.

If you give it some time and effort, and use this book to generate ideas on how to change your management style and your leadership model, then you will look forward to success far beyond that which the average enterprise will experience. You will be one of the winners in this new era.

When people ask me for just one word that describes what is most important in branding today, I have always answered 'Surprise!' in these last few years. A positive surprise, of course. And when people ask me what the outcome or result of branding is, I always answer 'consumer experience'. For me, customer experience and branding are almost the same thing... and both are very, very important for business success in any way you choose to measure it, whether it's profit or value creation for the owners.

And that's why customer experience branding is both the theme and the title of this new book that follows up on the very popular *4-D Branding*.

I have tried to make this book as practical and hands-on as possible, like my previous ones: a book for the new generation of business leaders and entrepreneurs.

Read and reap! I wish you enlightenment, encouragement and a good, inspiring read.

DEDICATION AND ACKNOWLEDGEMENTS

I would like to dedicate this book to all my customers/clients who over many years have inspired me to understand and develop customer experience branding, and who have given me the material for telling all the stories in this book. Many have become close personal friends in the process of us working together, and this has led to personal experiences and relationships that I value highly.

I also want to thank my loyal partner in life, Annette Rosencreutz, for her encouragement and ideas. Her enthusiasm inspired me to invest the time and effort that lie behind the creation of this book.

*'You've got to start with the customer experience
and work back toward the technology –
not the other way around.' Steve Jobs, 1997*

Introduction

Customer experience branding – surprise, surprise!

For business leaders today, customer experience matters the most: 89 per cent of the business leaders surveyed by Gartner believe that customer experience will be their primary basis for competition by 2016 and onwards (Gartner Inc, 2014).

The best way to understand what has happened with customer experience over the last 10–15 years is to look back and see what has happened with branding. Simply put, in today's world, with an increasing number of what I call 'relation brands', surprise becomes the most important differentiating element of success.

The classical idea of a brand used to be predictability. The first generation of brands were created as part of industrialism. Brands were supposed to always repeat themselves, mechanically. They were intended to predictably deliver, through their brand names or trademarks, an exactness of product, service benefit or experience to ensure that customers and users felt that they got exactly what they expected. Each time should be like the last time. This predictability for products and services was the primary customer experience.

McDonalds is a great example of this: wherever you are, and whenever you order it, a Big Mac should be the same. The fact that it is delivered with such exactness, always and everywhere in the world, allowed *The Economist* to create an international purchasing power parity called the Big Mac Index. An index that compares the same standardized product, with a typical mix of ingredients and production costs, in different countries.

All this was, of course, extremely important in a society that was making the change from mostly handcrafts to industrialism. Absolute predictability and reliability became the core reason for a customer to remember a trademark, and so predictability became the most important trait of any product or service brand.

Now, in our mature online culture, predictability is perceived as a basic characteristic of established brands, and is more or less taken for granted. We do appreciate it, but it doesn't excite us much. We have also learned that the fierce competitions in most categories of goods and services will negatively expose a non-reliable product or service; it will become a loser. The transparency of the internet, with reviews by interactive users, gives us even more confidence that a failure to continuously maintain quality will immediately become known to most consumers.

Modern brands have become purpose-oriented and multidimensional, with more perceived dimensions than merely the functional, such as social and individual, both mental and spiritual (see Chapter 6).

Positive surprises excite us

Since organized brands were first introduced over 100 years ago alongside industrialism, they have changed their nature and role in society. Brands are now becoming 'relation brands' – brands that have a greater effect on people than the functional, product-oriented delivery of tangible, predictable benefits and features.

Brands are built on perceptions and experiences, and branding can be defined as *managing perceptions and experiences in people's minds*. We are looking at different aspects of brands than we considered before. We like a brand to introduce us to new things. Brands should represent the future (or nostalgia), and make us feel updated and savvy. We want a brand to offer something that we proudly show off to friends; something that will become a new favourite.

The brand should be perceived a leader of its category. This gives us confidence in the brand, even when this isn't always true of its products or services. Some brands that are perceived as high innovation are not always first with the technology, but are first with exploiting a new user experience (like Apple and GoPro). It's even better if we can identify with the brand and feel that the brand is '*always reading my mind*', or that it's one step ahead of me or making me, as a customer, feel special and important. It's not just a different, new experience we're looking for, it's also the brand's personality. Again, this can be through a sense of nostalgia – when the brand is perceived as classic – or through following a new trend and being an agitator on the barricades of its category.

Customers already have very high expectations that the perceived top brands will be predictable in both their tangible deliveries and their personalities. I usually consider branding to be very similar to friendship, and positive surprises have always been a good way to maintain interest between friends. In fact, the same principle applies within any kind of relationship.

This becomes most challenging for strong brands. Since we love to be positively surprised by our favourite brands, the surprise-effect makes us more loyal. And when we are more loyal to brands, our friends and family take notice and are influenced by us. Even when we don't actually mention the brands in conversations, we are important promoters of the brands just by using them. We sometimes forget that.

When our favourite brands exceed the expectation we have of them, by giving us a surprise, we get more excited and our interest in and loyalty to the brand increases. One of the few things that makes us repeatedly loyal to a brand is experiencing something positively unexpected. And when a brand (and company) fails or vanishes from the market and our minds, it is usually caused by a lack of positive surprises for a long time. Surprises can become almost like a drug for us; the kick of the new and the different that we don't want to be without. When the time between the kicks of surprise gets longer and longer, we lose interest. This is why brands that fail to deliver those kicks have a very hard time. Especially if the brand had previously given their customers reason to anticipate surprising innovations.

We can look at Google to see this. The Google brand is continuously on the rise, always coming up with new surprises and out-of-the-box ideas like Google Glasses, driverless cars or singularity research and thought leadership with Ray Kurzweil. Even all the start-ups Google picks up create surprise, despite Google's prominent business strategy and its lead role in developing the digital world, the internet and mobile business. With Android, Uber, Waze, Nest and more, Google is continually surprising. Even the Google logo changes every so often, which a classic transaction brand would never do.

For contrast, we can turn to Apple. In the years following the death of Steve Jobs, the company's flow of surprises slowed to a stop. The perception of Apple as an innovative company that challenged the status quo and looked at the world in a different way began to fade. The result was that their relationship with their many fans and brand supporters showed signs reminiscent of a fading marriage. This was reversed when Apple introduced several new products and concepts at one very important launch event, almost two years after Steve Jobs' death.

Apple's example shows that these failing brands have the ability to recover again, but this kind of long-term disappointment and lack of surprise can lead to the loss of even the most loyal customers of a brand. Not every strong brand that was temporarily perceived as boring returns to the same dynamic strength it had before.

Personal surprises

The most important surprises are those that are presented in a personal manner. In Chapter 7 we'll look deeper into this and study what I call 'Easter egg surprises'. These are the surprises that we look forward to and anticipate, but are not sure that we'll get. At the very least, we want our anticipation to be confirmed, which itself creates a sense of surprise (see Chapter 7).

We like new surprises, ones that make the brand more human and personal, such as the pulsing light when the first generations of Apple's laptop computers were closed. Steve Jobs wanted it to mimic the beating of a human heart (Neylan, 2011).

It's of great importance for a relation brand to be perceived as personal. The tone of voice a brand uses today should be *surprisingly human*. The intuitive and proactive perception of the brand's nature has to become genuinely human. We're getting used to this now. The situation has matured and brands that don't have the right, human tone of voice are perceived, more than ever, as cold-hearted and unfriendly, and it becomes hard to build a relationship with them.

The other aspect of surprise

Positive, innovative and new experiences form one of two aspects that makes surprise important to the brands that have becomes successful in this new digital era: relation brands.

The other aspect is the mutability of these brands: the ability to change into something not initially anticipated. This change can come from within, when the brand managers choose to re-define it so that the brand stands for something new. The new perception develops gradually in the minds of people outside the organization.

With start-ups, this change of business and brand idea is called pivoting. It is usually caused by new discoveries about how users perceive the start-up's product or services and what their preferences are. Beta-testing the first version of a product usually results in a lot of customer feedback and this feedback often leads to changes in the product. Sometimes, these changes are huge and fundamental, such as when the feedback reveals that the customers want something very different from the product created by the founders of the start-up.

A change in brand strategy can be more, or less, dramatic. It can lead to a totally different brand, or just a slightly different one. It can be a difference caused by a change in the product or service, or by the product or service being introduced in different categories or market segments. It can also be simply a change in general perception, caused by factors like changing people's mind-set, without a great deal of tangible difference.

The most interesting change of brand perception is the one that takes place in the minds of a group outside the company, without help from the brand owners or managers. The brand owners are then just following up on the change in approach, product range or perception of the brand in people's minds.

Adidas is a good example of this. When the brand was in decline against its competitors and close to dramatically losing strength in the minds of traditional sports users and customers, the brand and its signature striped sportswear became a totally unexpected and cool way for urban teenagers in New York to express themselves. Adidas cleverly took advantage of this and amplified the classical brand, turning Adidas once again into a trendy brand. This led to a new perception of the Adidas brand among its traditional, core sport audience. Luckily, the brand owners didn't make the mistake of over-doing this positive change. Instead, they held off intervening too much and softly supported the process, playing along with it and gradually using it to restore the brand's position within its primary core market.

If you take a look at the most successful brands of the first 15 years of the 21st century – Facebook, Google, Apple, Starbucks, etc. (see 'Case book', page 000) – these brands were all initially unexpected, from a branding standpoint. Maybe this goes for business in general when introducing a new brand, but some new brands just follow up on already existing trends. In any case, it is certainly a truth in branding that the biggest successes are unexpected.

When many brands are set up, they anticipate certain things, like a certain target audience, a certain usage or having certain sought-after features and attributes. But in the end, the behaviour of customers and users that is not anticipated often becomes the most important factor. Either the way people use your product or service is not what you expected, or the aspects people prefer, like, or endorse about your brand are different from what you initially anticipated. One example of this, among many, is the Ford Mustang. It was originally created for young college students, but attracted mature men who liked to feel young and sexy. Even though the Ford Mustang's production costs were kept lower than the costs of most other cars, it remained too expensive for the college students.

A lot of brands have products and services that were supposed to be used in a certain way, but that were instead used in an unforeseen manner that turned out to be the real success for the brand. One example is Viagra, or sildenafil as it is officially known within the pharmacological industry. It was originally developed as a treatment for hypertension, angina and other symptoms of heart diseases. But while phase one clinical trials revealed that the drug wasn't great at treating the intended conditions, male test subjects experienced a rather unexpected side effect. A few years later, in 1998, the drug took the market by storm as a treatment for penile dysfunction, and became an overnight success. Between 2009 and 2013, Pfizer's annual financial reports list revenues of about $1.9 billion a year (Pfizer, 2016).

Another example of a brand and product where the attributes and features that were supposed to lead to success, didn't, is Coca-Cola. This icon of transaction branding was originally invented as an alternative to morphine addiction, and to treat headaches and relieve anxiety. Coke's inventor, John Pemberton, was a Confederate veteran of the Civil War who himself suffered from a morphine addiction due to his injuries (Agnew, 2013). He first invented Pemberton's French Wine Coca as a sweet, alcoholic drink infused with coca leaves. It would be another two decades before that recipe removed the alcohol and was honed, carbonated and, eventually, marketed into what it is today: still the most popular soda in the world.

In the modern start-up world, this phenomenon of designing something that is not used as planned, but instead becomes something else more successful, is called a pivot (a turn-around). A pivot is today considered a rather common and cool thing. Seasoned venture capitalists (VC) even talk about the importance of a start-up team having a 'plan B', because the experience in the VC world is that plan A seldom leads to success, but that the alternate plan B does. My opinion is that a pivot shouldn't be considered that cool. It actually represents a failure in finding out, first, what the customer needs and, second, what will be attractive and liked. Chapter 3 of this book deals with this.

References

Agnew, J (2013) *Alcohol and Opium in the Old West: Use, abuse and influence*, McFarland, Jefferson

Gartner Inc. (2014) Importance of customer experience on the rise – marketing is on the hook [Online] https://www.gartner.com/ [Last accessed: 20.1.16]

Neylan, C (2011) Apple's secret is in our DNA, all tech considered, 11/11 [Online] http://www.npr.org/sections/alltechconsidered/2011/08/30/140039539/apples-secret-is-in-our-dna [Last accessed: 20.1.16]

Pfizer (2016) Pfizer financial reports [Online] http://www.pfizer.com/investors/financial_reports/financial_reports [Last accessed: 20.1.16]

Branding

01

Managing perceptions in people's minds

The word 'branding' no longer properly describes what practitioners of branding mean today. Nor does it describe what they want the word to stand for.

It's the etymology of the word branding that gives the wrong impression. It comes from the language of my ancestors, the Vikings in Sweden, Norway, Denmark and Island. The Old Norse word 'brandr' (meaning 'to burn') referred to the practice of using a hot iron rod to impress the owner's markings or symbols (brands) on cattle, slaves, timber, crockery and more. This practice goes back as far as at least ancient Egypt.

What started as symbol of cattle ownership, warning potential thieves to keep their hands off, evolved over time into a sign of social, political and commercial inclusion. It became a marker of relationships, not just with the owner or producers, but also between people. Depending on context, brands can indicate practices, status, reputation and experiences. They can show relationships between producers, customers, consumers and opinion makers. They can describe quality, availability, price and service, as well as policies, personas, values, beliefs and the general allure of any political, social, commercial or cultural enterprise.

In addition, branding can be activated by a mix of production, service management, media choice, content creation, public relations, logistics and information technology, including social media.

In 2000 I founded the Medinge Group, a think-tank, with some of the world's leading new thinkers in branding. One of the first things we did was challenge the word branding, only to conclude, a few sessions later, that we could not actually find a better word to describe what branding stands for in our modern minds, despite all the wrong connotations. The good thing is that our brains recognize the word branding through pattern recognition (see Chapter 4). The history of a word is less important than what you make it into. In this sense, it's just the same as any brand that gets its value from what you make of it.

In this chapter I'd like to bring your attention to some aspects of branding that you may not have considered, which will help you manage your business.

Managing perception in people's minds

During all the years of my practice, by far the best definition of branding I have used is *'managing perceptions in people's minds'*. It tells us where the effect of branding takes place – in people's minds – and it tells us what that effect is – managing perceptions.

A good way to understand what branding does is to consider the opposite: what happens if you *do not use branding* at all? The amazing thing is that branding takes place anyway. But instead of the brand owner or manager intentionally guiding people, people use their imagination to fill the empty space, this vacuum of information, with their own ideas and fantasies.

This is always the case in situations when there is no available information; the empty space is filled with speculations, and the ideas based on them. People start to speculate, and share their speculations with others. Sometimes, outside commentators try to help by producing statements and comments, still without access to precise facts or real insight into the thinking of the decision makers.

I have never met, or heard of, any brand builders who found the right branding by launching their products with no planned branding effort. I have met their opposites, though, who complain that their brand is not perceived the way it should be, or that their brand is not in the forefront of people's minds as it is supposed to be. This is often the case with initially cocky brand owners who turn down offers of help with their branding strategy on the grounds that it would be a waste of time and money.

Managing is a key word in explaining what branding is all about. In most companies, there are many different management processes: human resources management, finance management, production management, procurement management, etc. Since branding is one of the most important processes in creating value, both in terms of equity and of the business's result (profit), it should definitely be considered an important core management process. Unfortunately, in most companies, it is not.

Sometimes this is the result of a traditional point of view. Branding is considered part of the marketing process, and yes, of course, it is an essential part of marketing. But there is much more to branding than just marketing; it is traditionally the basis of the company culture. Branding is usually where the company's vision, mission and values are stated. It is, simply, a sub-set of management strategy in any kind of enterprise, not just commercial. A favourite alternative phrase for branding is 'company DNA' or even 'company soul'.

Example: 'pirate branding' – how to manage perception of fear in people's minds

The marauding pirates of the Caribbean in the iconic pirate era of the 1650s to the 1720s are a very illustrative and dramatic example of effectively managing perception in people's minds. It begins with the 'logo' of the pirates: the classic flag most commonly attributed to Henry Avery, one of the most infamous pirate captains. The white skull in profile, wearing a kerchief, on a red or black background and with the crossed bones below very clearly depicts the fate of the crews who refused to surrender to the pirates.

An important part of managing the perception of a brand is being clear about what drives the brand owners – the *why* or the *purpose and mission* of the brand. A widespread myth states that the pirates were only interested in loot, and not in killing. This is why many ships full of merchandise, including gold and other valuables, surrendered relatively easily, with very little fighting. The sailors forced to fight by their ambitious navy officers knew very well that the pirates were outlaws with very little to lose, and that they were therefore extremely dangerous and brutal fighters. Many crews surrendered to pirates only to be recruited into pirate ranks, which not only kept them alive, but also offered monetary rewards. A pirate received one to two shares of the loot (Konstam, 2007) instead of the 19 to 24 shillings a month for a sailor offered by, for instance, the merchant navy (Hill and Ranft, 2002).

What comes first: business strategy or brand strategy?

Until a few years ago, my answer to the common question on how business strategy and branding strategy are related was that the business strategy comes first, because that is a 'long term plan of action designed to achieve a particular goal or set of goals or objectives' (Glykas, 2012). Making money is usually the main such goal. A business strategy is the management's game plan for strengthening the performance of the enterprise, including creating the business model and identifying the main customer target audience. Being only a brand advisor, I simply wanted to show a lot of respect for the other parts of the business.

Over the past few years, I have changed my mind about what comes first. I now promote the idea that the brand strategy comes first, and the business strategy or plan, including goals of performance and the business model, comes second. The reason for this change is that, in my practice and experience, I have seen too many businesses fail. Not because they haven't been able to come up with a very good business model and strategy for making money, but because they haven't been attentive enough to customer needs and customer perception.

In other words: an enterprise must address these wider and underlying customer needs, and come up with an idea, a concept and a customer experience that leads to a high level of customer acceptance. This acceptance, enthusiasm and loyalty results in a long-term relationship between the customer and the brand of the enterprise.

This last part is what a brand means today. If you research, develop and launch a business that does all this, you are almost guaranteed a success. There is a risk that setting up a business and trying to make money with a smart business model becomes the end in itself. Technology and development follows, with a little bit of made-up customer trailing behind, as opposed to thoroughly researching the customer experience.

Instead, begin with understanding the true customer experience. Who are the customers and users? What are their deeper needs? How do you ensure your customer experience has less friction and is more enjoyable when compared with existing alternatives? And how would that be perceived as different? Only when you understand the customer experience can you consider the technology and, finally or in parallel, look at how to combine the whole thing into a business with a good, smart business model.

Branding handles multiple stakeholder interests

Today's management teams are pushed by many different groups of stakeholders that become louder and more demanding all the time. They all want attention. And they all think they have should have access to the company leadership for information, strategy and answers to questions about everything in the business. As a leader, you tend to feel you have to give each of them an answer. They are customers, employees, shareholders, co-owners, retailers, dealers, suppliers, opinion makers, analysts... and competitors.

Figure 1.1 Why branding is even more important for business-to-business products or services

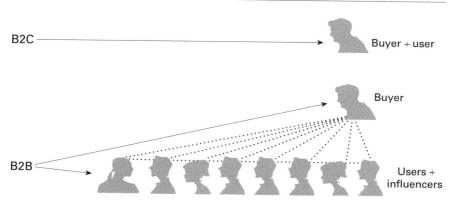

B2C ⟶ Buyer + user

B2B Buyer

Users + influencers

NOTE: B2C – business to customer; B2B – business to business

Normally, competitors are not included among stakeholders, but I maintain the odd idea that they are. Your competitors are usually better at describing your business than you are yourself. They are also the ones who can often sell your business and products or services better by comparing it with their own products or services. And sometimes they do it in a more interesting way than you and your own salespeople. Why is that?

It's because, in order to understand their own business and its unique selling point, they spend a lot of time and effort really looking at your strengths against theirs. And usually they are honest about your strengths, sometimes even impressed. They are able to very effectively describe who you are and why you are different, much quicker and more to the point that you can when you get lost in your own message. While you are being too complex, too worried about not forgetting every argument and detail of what you can deliver, they are able to focus on the essence of how your business differs from their own.

If you can deliver a very well-managed perception to all your stakeholders, including your competitors, that they can keep in their minds, remember and act upon, then you are on your way to a win. Since very few companies are able to do this, you will get rid of a lot of your competition simply by managing your perception better. I discuss the key elements of doing exactly that later in this chapter.

Branding offers a smarter entrance to the market

A smarter entrance to the market results in a higher rate of growth at lower costs. This sounds like a dream scenario, and it can be, but it is also an essential element for all business of all sizes, not just for small start-ups. It's about being more efficient, not only in production, logistics and time to market with innovations, but also in the way you reach into people's minds. In this area of marketing, there is a lot of waste.

Many businesses with good products and services are unable to convince people to even listen to them, let alone be interested and motivated to find out more about them. And on the other end of the scale, there are companies that are very good at creating attraction and truly engaging people with little effort. For almost no cost, they help build their business.

An interesting example of how a successful business uses customer experience branding and effective brand relations is the mobile network GiffGaff. The brand name is a Scottish word that means 'for mutual benefit'. The enterprise is a crowd-run venture wholly owned by O2, the UK operator that is now a part of Hutchinson Whampoa, the global telecom giant in Hong Kong.

GiffGaff was one of the later virtual operators to arrive on market, and it quickly became the third largest in this category. Launched as an experiment in 2009, it promised low prices, no contracts and fair treatment of customers. It typically texts members each month to tell them how to save money on their GiffGaff package. As a customer-driven organization, it operates more like a members' movement than a company. For instance, members who help other members gain free calls as a reward. You can read more about GiffGaff in 'Case book' (page 151).

The key elements of branding – and how to manage perceptions in people's minds

This is a short summary of the hands-on actions you can take to maximize your management of perception in people's minds. Each of these key elements is further explained in other chapters of the book. You can choose to read those sections now, or just read on and pick up the details as you go.

1 **Start with your higher intentions.** Describe, in as much detail as possible, what you want to achieve. Consider the big picture or your higher aim; your 'why' (Chapter 3) or your spiritual dimension (Chapter 6)

2 **Connect it to something people already know.** Consider how the part of the brain that makes decisions works (Chapter 4) and remember that it's a non-verbal part of the brain.

   Put simply, the brain asks these two questions before making a decision:

   - Have I seen this before? YES/NO
   - Was it a GOOD/BAD experience?

   Since the decision-making part of the brain is non-verbal, you need to use patterns to reach it.

3 **Create a pattern out of your perception.** Since the decision-making part of the brain is non-verbal, verbal communication and arguments do not have as great an impact on decisions as we have believed in the past. Visuals, activities (including enlisting existing customers as references and a sales force), processes, causality and similar approaches work better (Chapter 4).

4 **Connect with the individual.** Anything that is connected to the life and work of individuals is 70 per cent more effective in producing the desired perception in people's minds (Gabay 2015) (Chapter 4).

5 **Programme anticipation and prepare the surprise.** Use expressions like 'the first time ever', 'totally unique', 'different approach'. Announce an unexpected way of looking at this and tell the customer they will be surprised, then lift the lid off the 'Easter egg' (Chapter 7).

Conclusion: Branding is more than meets the eye for any business leader

In fact, branding is less of a strategy and more about tactics. In this chapter I want to start by disrupting the idea of the opposite. Branding should be understood as one of the top management systems needed to run a successful business. It should help any business leader, or owner, to manage the way others outside and inside their business look at them. Branding includes a way to manage stakeholder information interests, to establish the product or service of a business in the minds of people and to protect these from being copied and used by competitors. Branding is also a natural way to accelerate the marketing, to create a better launch and shorten the time to market.

The brand perception is key to creating a successful brand, and a successful brand is key to a business gaining even greater success. Perception is setting the expectations, and fulfilling them. When expectations are not fulfilled, there is no positive customer experience. In this way, your brand guides customers to see and experience what you want them to.

This is the why I always advocate that a business should start with the brand, preferably prior to building the business strategy, but at least in parallel with it. The brand is fundamental to setting the most important part of a business strategy – the relationship with the customers. All my experience shows that if you start at that end – the customer end of the business journey – you will be much more likely to produce a positive result than if you start with just the business strategy. Therefore, we will return to the customer, and to the customer experience, many times throughout this book.

References

Gabay, J (2015) *Brand Psychology: Consumer perceptions, corporate reputations*, Kogan Page, London

Glykas, M (ed) (2012) *Business Process Management: Theory and applications*, Springer, Heidelburg

Hill, JR and Ranft, B (2002) *The Oxford Illustrated History of the Royal Navy*, Oxford University Press, Oxford

Konstam, A (2007) *Scourge of the Seas: Buccaneers, pirates and privateers*, Osprey Publishing, Oxford

Relation brands 02

How the internet introduced surprise branding

Since the internet became more accessible at the beginning of the 1990s, it has changed branding at least as much as industrialism did, and industrialism's mass production and mass marketing changed branding forever. The internet has become breakthrough technology, in much the same way as the steam engine was for industrialism. In many ways, this new change has proven to be more dramatic than just a change in communication channel. Being inside the media itself gives it more influence on society and our way of thinking than other technologies. It has even changed the message of branding.

The most interesting part is that this change shows clear spiral qualities. In this spiral development, the internet has taken branding back to the point on the horizontal plane where it had traditionally been before industrialism – back to the relationship between the maker of a product or service and the buyer and user. But on the vertical level, it has elevated this to a higher plane. The limitations of a physical personal relationship have been eliminated through internet technology that has created a relationship economy of scale, just as industrialism created a production economy of scale.

The change this new relation branding causes cannot be emphasized enough. It is seen not only in marketing, but also in the way a modern business is run. It is a fundamental shift in both our perception of what is happening and in the way we act on the change. In my experience as a business advisor, I still see how many businesses are struggling with understanding and acting on this paradigm change, even though it's now a developed part of our business lives.

That struggle is why this book is needed: to introduce a new perspective, a new approach and a new toolbox, that will permeate most business processes and touch on almost every company detail. In many ways, it substantially changes the way most companies are managed. So, let's take a brief look at some of these effects. Throughout this book, we'll learn how to manage the impact of relation branding within the company structure and business processes. What follow are some of the most important characteristics of relation branding.

Meaning is the essence of relation brands

As discussed in 'Notes', transaction brands sprang from industrialism and its commercial consumer culture. The focus was on the material benefits for consumers and users. Industry produced new products using economies of scale. Mass marketing these products was part of the whole and advertising became a way of creating the model for the new consumers. The message was either highly product orientated, pragmatic about the features of the product or service, or a combination of material and social satisfaction, in terms of status and the endorsement of the cool, savvy consumer. Sometimes this was strengthened by celebrities in the role of super-consumer.

With relation brands, we see something else: the search for a deeper meaning in consuming. We see how successful new companies are built on a foundation of creating meaning for consumers. When Guy Kawasaki (ex-Apple Macintosh executive and start-ups investor) lectures for entrepreneurs, he challenges them to create meaning:

> the core, the essence of entrepreneurship is about making meaning... those companies that are fundamentally founded to change the world, to make the world a better place, to make meaning, are the companies that make a difference. They are the companies to succeed... if you make meaning, you will probably make money. But if you set out to make money, you will probably not make meaning and you won't make money.

(Kawasaki, 2004)

In his book and lectures, Guy Kawasaki explains how you can create meaning in three ways: first, you can increase quality of life; second, you can right a wrong – you find something that's wrong that you want to fix; third, you can prevent the end of something good – you see something beautiful and just can't stand the fact that it's being changed or eroded.

Relation brands are obviously about creating relationships. As we'll soon see, it's basically the same as creating friendships. In these friendships, you need to find something to share, something that goes beyond the surface, something with meaning.

The large-scale individualization that the internet brings to us with economy of scale needs relationships and friendships that accelerate the demands of mutual commitment: 'if I buy, and am loyal to, your brand's quality products or services, I anticipate that you will not only satisfy my functional needs, but also give me something meaningful along with it'. This is the unspoken reasoning of today's consumer, further dramatized by official ecological, ethical and social responsibility demands in today's world, along with the massive threat to our quality of life from climate changes produced by our reckless consumption and increased CO_2 pollution.

Meaning cannot be compromised for a modern brand. The question is how to manage the situation, and how to shift from the earlier focus on convenience and quality, to instead embrace the complicated world around us and make this complexity fundamental for a profitable business. This is precisely the management challenge in today's companies. And here, modern branding serves as good tool. By understanding the nature of the relation brand, you have a model for handling the general leadership challenges of today, and beyond.

I asked Grant McCracken, consumer sociologist and writer of *Culture and Consumption II: Markets, meaning and brand management* (2005) for his thoughts on the challenges of branding for today's managers, with regard to purpose and meaning. His answer follows:

I think the biggest issues in branding are:

1 Learning the old mechanics of meaning management through branding: how we make meanings for the brand, meanings in the consumer needs, meanings in what the consumer build into his/her own life.

2 Learning the new meaning management through branding, now that we have new media (internet, mobile phones, etc) and more consumer participation (co-creation, etc).

3 Learning how to manage complexity. New brands have to be more things to more people. That means managers need to know how to manage a much bigger and more complicated bundle of brand meanings.

(McCracken, 2011)

Friendship branding

Friendship is key to understanding and mastering a relation brand. We all have people in our lives that we regard as friends. That makes it easier to simply consider your friends and act the same way towards your brand as you would towards your friend. Friendship has high social expectations – if you forget to call on a friend's birthday, you're in trouble. It's the same with relation branding; the expectations are very high. If you forget to pay attention to your customers and your brand community, you are out.

Relation branding is, in many ways, more demanding and more difficult than transaction branding. But if you look at it in terms of a personal friendship, rather than from a business point of view, it becomes much more natural.

You have to call in once in a while to gossip with your friends. It's the same with relation branding. That's why emailing, tweeting, blogging and Facebooking become critical for many individuals.

We also need *surprise*. We know the effect surprise has on a friendship. And it's the same with all types of relationship. Imagine a friend unexpectedly surprising you with tickets to the game or a show or, even better, suggesting that you go on a trip together, fishing or travelling somewhere you both want to go. Doing things together, having a common interest or purpose, are monumental brand-building initiatives that improve a relation brand in exactly the same way they improve a friendship.

Storytelling and customer involvement

When we start looking at how the concept of marketing has changed with relation branding, and with the availability of new media technologies, we see that the change here is a very dramatic one. Marketing was created to solve industrialism's mass production problem of how to create a market to offset the new, vast quantities of products produced by cost-efficient industries. Products that didn't exist prior to industrialisation, or that weren't accessible to most people, needed a market. New techniques of cataloguing consumers, like segmentation and target group definitions, were invented to find the right consumers for the right products in strict economic, transaction terms.

New methods of communicating were also created as part of marketing, including terminology like USP, the unique selling proposition. The idea was that every product and service needed to find and communicate its reason-to-be to its customer or user. The focus was squarely on the functional, rational and relevant elements in this first era of marketing. Since some products were true inventions, consumers were sold first on their functionality. Gradually, over time, the indirect effects of the products were communicated. And in the latest phase of pure transaction branding, the life situation, or lifestyle, connected with the product came into focus.

By the 1970s, the advertising of most products was much more about the external lifestyle, image and status than about the efficiency of the product itself (Kurtuldu, 2012). Some products remained in the first phase, communicating direct tangible benefits, and in many cases these products continue to do this. It is still important. Transaction brands and their products or services live side by side with relation brands.

This can sometimes be confusing: that some of today's products retain this late transaction brand social status focus, and remain connected to image-communication, but now bring it to a much deeper and more personal and integrated level. It becomes a symbolic signal device in a complex social context. More than just a stand-alone product admired by your peers, some brands' products have become important props in people's lives, functioning like props in a movie, to manifest a customer's or user's personality.

The future of marketing relation brands is obviously very much about how to use the social networks of the internet and mobile devices, such as YouTube, Instagram, Pintrest, Google+, Facebook and LinkedIn. All these networks are prime examples of relation brands themselves. By studying the development of these social media platforms, it's easier to see how modern relation brands should be managed with a high level of user participation.

The centrepiece of relation branding is the story. This includes not only the story of the product brand, but also the story of the founders' personal brands. These stories can, of course, be very different, but one common ingredient is the founders' passion for the brand and the business. The pursuit, mission, meaning and purpose with which they differentiate themselves while creating the brand, are more important today than ever before.

Daniel Ek, founder and CEO of Spotify, exemplifies this. As with many other entrepreneurs, his own personal brand is integrated with the brand of the company he founded. His personality, passion, drive and purpose, his whole life at large, including his success story, are public and part of the company brand.

The other significant aspect about marketing a relation brand is the authentic involvement of the consumer in the business. Some transaction brands have also liked activating their audiences. However, for the most part this activation is in the marketing only; the consumers are kept at a certain distance from the business. In relation branding, the involvement of the customers is much deeper.

It can start with co-creation or co-evaluation, and include participation in producing content, as with the users of GoPro. Facebook, along with many other social-oriented services or apps, offers individuals a much deeper involvement in the creation of the product. Another very deep integration between the brand and the buyers and users of a product is crowdfunding; a combination of being investor and customer at the same time.

One example of many successful crowdfunding projects is Pono. This iPod-like music device delivered a sound far better than any that existed before, with exception of the recorded sound track itself. Pono's fundraising on KickStarter, one of the first of the crowd sourcing platforms, was record-breaking, with many enthusiastic first customers who also acted as investors now taking delivery of 'their' product.

Even more traditional businesses, like the automotive industry, offer interesting opportunities for co-creation. The 'mini people' – fans of the Mini Cooper – paint and individualize their cars, meet on regular basis, parade down the road to and from their meets, and create a lot of attention for the brand. Customers can also act as brand ambassadors, passionately communicating the latest gossip and information about new products to be released.

Sometimes this interaction and involvement is so intimate that understanding who is leading the process can be difficult. This becomes a problem when your ambition is to manage relation brands; it's certainly not like pushing buttons, which was the idea with the mechanically inspired transaction branding. You need patience and a sixth sense for human interactions, relationships and communications to master this. The outcome can be very impressive in commercial terms, but the process usually takes a light hand, intuition, modesty, and 'selling by not selling'. The goal is to create a lot of free, non-pushy creative content, in order to attract attention, and create surprise and long-term relations. This kind of management, without pushiness, can be very stressful, especially in larger enterprise structures that demand short-term profit.

Passionate brand ambassadors

These are the backbone of a relation brand's sales organisation. This is in absolute contrast to the 'pushy, arguing product politician' typical of the transaction brand sales structure that relies on a hired sales force tasked with convincing the consumer of the product's value, in the same way as politicians argue for their party. Relation brand ambassadors love the brand story and are willing to tell everyone, at every opportunity. And they do it peer-to-peer, in conversation, not speaking from a podium.

These brand ambassadors are an important cause of the success of π relation brands. They are also one of the reasons why these new types of brands can do so much with so much less advertising, even none at all. So, a major marketing task for a relation brand is not the hard sell that pushes their brand, but understanding and identifying with the customer in a new way. The techniques of selling become the opposite of selling: a softer, more interactive, socially networking kind of conversation. In Chapter 10, when we look into the sales process, we'll look into how a modern relation branding company can turn this into an art form and a business process in itself.

Small ideas in combination and constant improvement

The innovation process is another example of how relation brands differ from the typical transaction brands. Transaction brands focus on the product and always try to challenge that product, silently, in their research.

Relation brands instead understand that the innovation process is part of the storytelling, and work to keep the story alive and supply new information to brand ambassadors. When launching entirely new products, a relation brand can use many, small, existing ideas and technologies and create a new, interesting and uniquely perceived product that addresses customer needs. Design is an important ingredient in this pursuit of creating visible differentiation while supporting the story of the passionate, entrepreneurial spirit of innovating.

It is more important for a relation brand to maintain a dialogue with its customers, and to respond to customer needs with new features and constant improvements, than it is to challenge their existing products. If the innovation process for a transaction brand is somewhat 'paranoid', always trying to challenge classic hero products, the innovation process for a relation brand is not without stress.

For a relation brand, the constant flow of new products or the development of existing ones is very important. The relationship needs to be fed with news constantly. The conversations within the brand fan network must never fade out, but must always be fuelled with news and other conversation pieces. The brand story must be constantly invigorated. This is the pressure of the relation brand. The good news is that the innovations can be evolutionary, rather than revolutionary (even if they are sometimes dramatized in the storytelling to seem revolutionary).

Peer to peer: Engaged and democratic

We can conclude that the behaviour of relation brands differs from transaction brands through their deep social connections with their audiences. These audiences are typically not only customers, but include anyone who could be helpful in creating the brand. Stakeholders include opinion makers, reviewers or bloggers, suppliers and, as we have seen, the brand's competitors themselves. We have probably all experienced absurd moments when a brand seems to be selling another competitor better than it is selling itself. Another aspect of this important widening of the branding perspective is that the relation brand can recruit new staff members from competitors and suppliers.

As already mentioned, the tone of voice of a relation brand is different from the tone of transactions brands. The attitude is also different. For most relation brands, friendship is the formula for the relation. You treat your customers and all your stakeholders as friends or partners; opening up the development of the relationship makes the brand more trustworthy and authentic, more like a peer, more democratic and engaged. All these are very important for a modern brand.

Brands have been built using being green, sustainable and responsible as a way to create a deeper and more engaged relationship, leading to further involvement. In recent years, we have seen how sustainability is becoming increasingly political correct and a standard, and expected, part of most brands. We have seen how these expected things – predictability, quality and sustainability – are taken for granted, and therefore they become less important for brand differentiation and brand success.

For most transaction brands this was very uncomfortable, irrelevant and a distraction from the core of the product or service. The story of Bellissimo, the producer of Swiss Noir chocolate, is a good example. In a world where 'fair trade' is becoming a huge topic, Bellissimo sued the small, Dutch, 'slave-free' chocolate producer, Tony's Chocolonely in 2007, for implying that all other chocolate is produced using slave labour. Bellissimo lost the case, since the journalist who started Tony's Chocolonely could produce enough evidence supporting his claim, and they also lost some of their market share due to the negative PR. As a traditional Transaction Brand, Bellissimo did not anticipate the critical relationship between a product and more important issues in people's minds.

A good relation brand creates partnerships between its stakeholders, becoming a vehicle in pursuit of creating a better world. The cause has to be at least slightly unexpected and unusual to create interest among groups of brand fans. As consumers, we are simply looking for brands with meanings and purposes that we can make our own, and thereby differentiate ourselves. One of the greatest drives is to be differentiated, yet socially part of something interesting.

Conclusion: A new type of brand and a new brand strategy is needed

The internet and digital communications have changed the world and our human behaviour more than any other technology in the last 100 years. A new tool box is needed for management to handle this new paradigm, along with a new approach to branding. In fact, a new type of brand has appears that I call a relation brand. Built on a pattern of relationships, relation brands began to be seen around 2000 and they are a very different type of brand when compared to the traditional transaction brands that focused on the product or service itself.

One of the strategic tools that now needs to be different is meaning: a brand now needs to help create a better world for us, rather than just support more shopping. The commercial aspect still exists in relation branding, but the brand is about much more than the just the product or service. It also includes and relates to many other aspects of life, such as meaning, sustainability, humanism, quality of life, tolerance, innovation and change. This book is a handbook for the new world that these values and this type of brand will shape.

References

Kawasaki, G (2004) *The Art of the Start: The time-tested, battle-hardened guide for anyone starting anything*, Portfolio, New York

Kurtuldu, M (2012) Brand new: The history of branding [Blog] *Design Today*. 29/11. [Online] http://www.designtoday.info/brand-new-the-history-of-branding/ [Last accessed: 25.1.16]

McCracken, G (2005) *Culture and Consumption II: Markets, meaning and brand management*, Indiana University Press, Bloomington

McCracken, G (2011) Personal interview

Embracing the unexpected   03

A new kind of business strategy

As Nassim Nicholas Taleb told us in his book *The Black Swan* (2007), humans have a tendency to find simplistic explanations for highly improbable, rare and unpredictable events. A black swan was an impossible creature, until one was discovered. And it's much the same with the branding. How the product is used and which features and attributes are most important are often impossible to know, until they are shown. That is why most entrepreneurs, inventors and marketers are in for surprises. Sometimes these are good, positive and prosperous surprises. Sometimes, unfortunately, they are quite the opposite. Those are the ones we know very little about; they are seldom discussed. That's the nature of things.

Socrates famously said, 'I know one thing: that I know nothing.' This, along with Oscar Wilde's 'To anticipate the unexpected shows a thoroughly modern intellect' (*An Ideal Husband*, 1895) is an important part of developing a new kind of business strategy. We need to modernize our attitudes towards unexpected branding and open our minds to the fact that the best way of creating a strong brand is not something you can plan and foresee. Only by embracing the probabilities of the unexpected can you be really successful.

We don't just need to be prepared for the downside of the unexpected (as is mostly the case with Taleb's black swan). This kind of risk-minimizing is most interesting for financial investors and insurance executives. As brand leaders, we also need to embrace, or learn to love, the unexpected in order to facilitate the creation of the unexpected brand. Becoming more sharing, more open to new ideas and unexpected innovations often leads to better branding. It is the expansive upside that we look for with customer experience branding and positive surprises.

Now, you may feel that this is the final nail in the coffin of brand strategy. And you are partly right! It is the final nail for the old school of brand strategy: transaction brand strategy. This kind of strategy is part of old mechanistic, industrial, mass-market thinking, focused only on product or service based branding. Attentive to customers only collectively, as target groups with clearly outspoken, clichéd needs, ignoring the deeper and weaker signals from individual minds and the experiences of individual consumers and users.

For the relation brand strategy, it's just a beginning. This is the modern brand strategy, built on individual relationships between the brand itself and the customers, consumers and users of the product or service. This branding is anchored in the sharing and reviewing of an idea with the ambition of a higher purpose and meaning.

The products and services are just part of this idea, not the whole of the idea. This means that customers and users are part of this brand strategy, and are invited to share their experience and co-create, or at least co-evaluate. It's a brand strategy that truly opens the brand up for the unexpected.

Customer experience driven business and branding strategy

This is the start of a new type of business and branding strategy, driven by customer experience. In fact, the old business strategy doesn't fit into the new scenario. Instead of a strategy prepared to exclude and deny things that might happen along the way, the new strategy opens up and accepts the possibilities. Classical business strategy feels like a contradiction of the concept of strategy we have come to know by building businesses in uncertainty.

In the industrial paradigm, uncertainty was unacceptable. The classical approach to business strategy was to carry on as if you know you are right in all your assumptions. While engineers in most industries today accept the fact that the product has to change if users and customers don't like what is produced, fundamentally, the classical business strategy as a concept has not changed. It is still very inflexible and classical brand strategy has followed that inflexibility.

The new way of looking at business strategy follows the ideas of lean management. It should be set up as a living, developing, document – like a hypothesis in science – as something preliminary to be iterated. The strategy is then put into practice in real situations, like a beta-version with real customers and users. The concept has to be proven, adjusted and changed.

The roles of the new business strategy

The new type of business strategy plays several important roles in setting up the business:

1 The first role of the new business strategy is to tap in to the minds of a smaller number of representatives of the potential customers and users. This research, called business ethnography or business anthropology, is based on customer experience and includes reading the weaker signals and user patterns. The idea is to research customer and user experiences in depth, unfiltered by your own ideas as an entrepreneur and your desired customer response. By seeing what is there, rather than your preferred reality, this research produces unexpected and surprising results.

2 The second role of the new business strategy is the strategy itself: coming up with a different, exciting, new, yet practical idea for how to do things, whether through a product or a service.

   The input here obviously begins with your own creative ideas on how to use new technology or science to create something better than that which currently exists. But you must also bring in the ideas and nuances in functionality, usability, communication and more that resulted from your business ethnography research in step 1. The next question regards the resources needed, and the costs required.

   Because this idea is hypothetical and likely to be adjusted and changed, it can be more daring, different and surprising than you might first have considered. So, from the beginning, we have an opportunity to build something unexpected. As long as it remains relevant to most of the customer signals and patterns of thinking, and rests firmly on a base of customer experience.

3 The third role of the new business strategy is to test-launch the product or service and sample the customers' experiences of both buying and using it, including the Net Promoter Score question: 'Would you recommend this to your friend?' (We study Reichheld's Net Promoter Score in greater detail in Chapter 9.)

   This is the point at which you fine-tune or change your business strategy so that it fits with the most important customer and user experiences. You may choose to add non-mainstream usage patterns or ideas, or even accept an odd and surprising way of using your product or service that is still relevant to your user needs.

4 The fourth role of the new business strategy is the continuation of the business project, including sub-strategies that cover how to reach potential customers. Here, you also need to adjust an account for potential customers you didn't foresee. This step is in addition to the normal testing of channels, messages and offers. You can also set up a programme of surprises, which could include new products, features, technologies, usage, markets, applications and combinations with other businesses and brands. It may even be desirable to appoint a CSO – chief surprise officer (see Chapter 11).

Integrating brand strategy and business strategy

In this new approach, the brand strategy is an integrated part of the overall business strategy, where the brand strategy manages the perceptions and experiences in people's minds. This means that the brand will always interact with product development, with sales and marketing activities and with the customer experience. Simon Sinek has brilliantly described the *why*, *how* and *what* in a TED talk in 2009, 'How great leaders inspire action'.

This new brand strategy uses the definition of branding as managing perception in people's minds. It begins with finding out what is in the mind of the customer or user, but it also needs the context of what is happening in the world, related to your product or service category. This comes before the product, before the content, before the business strategy that acts as the road map of how to make this user-based idea successful as a business.

To become a successful entrepreneur, you now have to begin with the *why* – define the purpose and the change needed in the world, narrowed done to the category of product, services or experiences. In step two, you begin finding out *how* people are thinking with regard to that category – what is important for them, what do they need, what must be changed or improved? Based on the customer needs and experiences, you can create your ideas and strategies for the brand. It will then be the perfect result of tapping into the minds of people and their life context. It will be based on how existing problems and challenges can be solved and on how to create a better, more meaningful, life for users.

In the third step, you have the base to approach *what* you are going to do about it. Whether you introduce new technologies and sciences, transfer experiences from one business category to another or are inspired by innovations in other areas of human life, you can create a truly new product, service or solution that exactly meets unsolved customer and user needs.

The great advantage of starting with *why* something needs to be changed in the world is that you focus on something with a higher level of meaning from the outset. This saves you from trying to solve problems that are not essential, and from not differentiating your product or service sufficiently against your competitors'.

When you the look at the *how*, you can create a product that becomes a favourite among your customers and users that they will readily recommend to others. By basing your product or service on the WHY, on the higher purpose and meaning, you become not just another salesperson, desperately seeking customers for your product. Instead, you are already different, more interesting and more in tune with what customers need, envision and imagine in their dreams.

How a very young entrepreneur did what established international businesses couldn't

George Edwards was only 19 years old when I first met him. We met over dinner in London and he amazed me with his story. He had invented a way to measure the content in a gas bottle. Companies like AGA, Linde and AirLiquide, a whole established and profitable industry with all the technical and scientific resources imaginable, had never been able to measure, and tell the users as well as themselves as suppliers, how much was left in the gas tank. The only way to determine this was to lift the tank and feel how heavy it was, or to shake it and guess at how much remained.

Customers everywhere had the same needs and interest in knowing it was time to replace the gas bottle, or if enough remained to cook the Sunday roast in the mobile home, caravan or boat. Without being able to tell how much remained, users only had a choice between being safe and using the spare bottle now, or waiting and seeing if the old one lasted.

By tapping the minds of gas customers and users, and studying their needs at caravan campsites and boat clubs, George also discovered another need. His future customers had no way of telling if their gas system was leaking: a safety issue, of course.

He started to develop a technical solution and created an algorithm for smartphones that calculated and predicted gas consumption based on the individual consumer's usage patterns. Someone who uses gas bottles for their kitchen stove has a very different consumption pattern than someone who uses the garden gas-grill now and then. The input for the algorithm is relayed wirelessly to the smartphone from a magnetic strip on the side of the gas bottle, using Bluetooth. When he was ready to launch his 'Gas-Sense' product, George created a crowdfunding Kickstarter campaign to raise money to manufacture the first batch. When I saw the list of people who sent him money in advance to get first delivery of the product, it was clear that they were from all over the world. The obvious conclusion was that anything less than a world launch would be inappropriate.

Before we began working together on his brand strategy, he told me something very important: he had four other inventions in mind. And he had used the same methodology to get the ideas for these. He had, first, observed and tapped into people's minds, and then considered how to meet their needs in a new way, using new technology and science, by transferring business patterns from other fields of business. The steps in the brand boot camp for start-ups are described in detail in Figure 8.3 (page 000).

Do companies fail if they don't disrupt themselves first?

Ever since Clayton Christensen wrote his book *The Innovator's Dilemma* in 1997, it has been accepted as a fact that companies will fail if they don't disrupt themselves first.

Lately there have been attacks on this nice template for business innovation. The first was from Jill Lepore, a Harvard historian who took issue with Christensen's book, and with the whole circus of innovation consultants and conferences that arose from it. In an article for *The New Yorker* she described disruptive innovation as 'a competitive strategy for an age seized by terror' (Lepore, 2014). A number of members of academia have followed up on this by pointing out that not all the disrupters Christensen lauded survived, and not all the disrupted incumbents disappeared.

The lesson of this discussion is simply that generalized rules for innovation strategy do not seem to apply, as Peter Diamandis shows. Described by *FT* as 'the self-appointed high-priest of digital disruption' and co-author of the book *Bold* (Diamandis and Kotler, 2015), he coined the idea that a bold entrepreneurial strategy has to be based on a vision of exponential growth. By his reasoning, 'linear' organizations are doomed. However, he created XPrise in 1996 in order to encourage privately funded space travel, and it has still not exponentially taken off, whatever Peter Diamandis may believe.

At the same time, a bold incumbent does not always have to destroy its core business to survive. The boldest companies, new or long established, are the ones with a forward-looking policy of constant innovation and creativity based on genuine interest in the early warnings and weak signals from users and customers. A strategy that can lead to innovation, instead of glancing over their shoulders at competitors.

Conclusion: How to turn the unexpected to your business and branding advantage

The first step towards not fearing the unexpected but instead embracing it is to be aware of it. Here, we can learn from Nassim Nicholas Taleb and his unexpected black swan. But it's important to keep in mind that there is usually much more to the unexpected than the downside. The upside of being receptive to the unexpected is that it becomes easier to turn the unexpected into a positive management strategy instead of a crisis.

The new method of building strategy begins with brand thinking and customer focus. Ensuring that a business survives takes constant innovation and creativity based on a genuine interest in the early warnings and weak signals from users and customers. Following these signals, instead of looking over your shoulder at competitors and desperately trying to disrupt the business, can lead to innovation in itself. Taking risks is a way for a business to always take the position to win, yet identifying worthy risks, and not taking unnecessary ones, is the key to success. In the next chapter we look at how new research into how the brain works can help you identify what is a worthy risk and what is not.

References

Christensen, C (1997) *The Innovator's Dilemma: When new technologies cause great firms to fail*, Harvard Business School Press, Boston

Diamandis, PH and Kotler, S (2015) *Bold: How to go big, create wealth and impact the world*, Simon & Schuster, New York

Lepore, J (2014) The disruption machine: What the gospel of innovation gets wrong, *The New Yorker*, 23 June [Online] http://www.newyorker.com/magazine/2014/06/23/the-disruption-machine [Last accessed 29.1.16]

Taleb, NN (2007) *The Black Swan: The impact of the highly improbable*, Random House, New York

Branding brain   04

How new research about the brain can help create surprises

The expression in this chapter's title, 'Branding brain', is similar to Nokia's 'Connecting people'. It carries a double meaning. It can either refer to how the brain is instrumental in branding (collectively), or it can refer to branding the brain (individually) with 'personal branding'. In this book we cover both aspects. The latter is discussed in Chapter 15 and we discuss how the brain works together with branding here.

Surprise findings

Since about 2005, neuroscientists have monitored the brain to discover exactly how it works. Modern scanning technology has tracked the signal and shown how data flows in our brains. Neuroscientists can now clearly see how the different sections are connected and how they interact when we act and think.

How our brains make decisions has been a popular research area. Here, neuroscientists act as hardware experts in a tech company, while psychologists are software and user experience experts. Today, they work together to provide a synchronized view on how the brain actually works.

For a long time, before sophisticated brain scanning, we categorized decision making into two types of decision: rational and emotional. When psychologists began studying the human mind, it was assumed that humans are rational creatures. Consequently, for many years the importance of the conscious brain and rational decisions have been heavily emphasized.

However, to understand the impact neurological research has had on branding, we must understand that the great focus we have always had on verbal communication is not enough to attract the attention of the decision maker in our brains. We've been living with the idea that verbal arguments substantially impact decision making, and that pure facts and logic can attract the necessary attention and convince and change people's minds. From experience, we now know that this is not the way forward. How, then should we act?

The non-conscious brain drives behaviour

We often can't explain why we do what we do, why we decide what we decide, or how we will behave in the future. This is because most of our behaviour is driven by our non-conscious brain, which we can't access. This casts a lot of questions over the conclusions we derive about consumer behaviour from what people tell us in research studies.

We experience the world through patterns. Our unique experiences build patterns that explain how the world works and we store these patterns as neural networks in the brain. Because our experiences are all unique, even when we experience the same event as others, our patterns are all different. And it is these patterns that greatly influence our behaviour and how much attention we pay to different things when making decisions.

Our brains evolved to constantly scan our environment and ensure that there is nothing life threatening nearby. For this reason, new or unexpected things that don't fit into the expected pattern capture our attention (Weinschenk, 2011). Neuroscience studies have shown that our brains not only look for the unexpected, they crave it (Berns, 2001). Our brains look for patterns and try to match those patterns with anything that is already stored in our memory. When the patterns match, the neural networks are strengthened and our views become more entrenched. When they don't match, the brain re-calibrates and stores new patterns. Brains are built to generate predictions, and this ability to predict is the basis for problem-solving.

The neocortex uses memories to make predictions, measures what actually happens against these memories and records the difference. When we solve problems, the brain doesn't compute the answer, it retrieves the solution from memory and the vast majority of our brains' predictions happen outside of our awareness (Hawkins, 2004).

The non-conscious brain makes decisions

Our brains are designed to take conscious information and to turn it into non-conscious experiences. Driving a car is a simple example of this. We first learn to drive consciously, reminding ourselves of every step until it becomes second nature. At this point it becomes non-conscious. This allows our brain to think consciously about other things while we are driving.

Our non-conscious brain has over 200,000 times more processing capacity than our conscious brain. And still it can't handle the increasing amounts of information coming at us from the world around us. Therefore, our brains create shortcuts, many of which may mislead us (Dijksterhuis et al, 2009). Our non-conscious brain is deeply empirical; it learns from its past experiences and mistakes (Hawkins, 2004). Brand builders and marketers need to consider this dominant, non-conscious brain in decision making.

When we need to make a decision, the non-conscious brain assesses the alternatives, generates a positive or negative feeling based on its conclusion, and sends that feeling to the conscious brain. Our non-conscious brain has already completed a detailed analysis and advises us what to do, for everything from complex purchase decisions like buying a car to mundane ones like choosing a breakfast cereal. By the time our conscious brain reacts, the non-conscious brain has already analysed thousands of variables: how expensive each cereal is, how healthy each is, whether we recognize them, whether we have eaten them before, and if so what we thought of them, whether we've seen ads for them and what message we took away from these ads.

Our conscious mind can make better choices when there are only a few choices and not very many variables. However, our world is filled with too many variables and choices to allow our brain to store all the details of everything we experience. When things become too complex, the non-conscious brain takes over to make better and quicker decisions.

Relationships are remembered before details

Over the millions of years of our evolution, our brains have put more emphasis on storing relationships between events, emotions, causes and effects than on storing the details of memories. The brain doesn't care about accuracy or detail. Its purpose is to help us make decisions in the future, and our memories are notoriously inaccurate. With so many memories and experiences stored in our brains, we can only remember a few at a time. And since the brain holds onto the relationships between things rather than the details, it creates details when it needs them, building them from other memories, cultural norms and expectations, filling in the gaps to create a complete story (Gilbert, 2006).

This attention to relationships helps us learn things by rote, like the alphabet or the months of the year. It also explains why it is not as easy to quickly recite the alphabet backwards, or list the months from December to January. For brand owners, it's important to remember this and create marketing content that relies on relationships between things, rather than on the details. Structuring the content in a sequence is one of several effective ways of helping people remember the message you want to deliver (Hawkins, 2004).

Breaking patterns and forming new ones

Recent brain research supports the idea of breaking patterns and introducing new information in a crisis situation. Neurobiological research shows that even powerful memories, such as fear conditioning, can be altered or eradicated by inhibiting the neural mechanism during the retrieval of the memory. This suggests that the retrieval stage of the memory is an active and dynamic relearning process rather than a mere replay of previously acquired information (Schafe et al, 2001).

Decisions are emotional, not logical

When professor and neuroscientist Antonio Damasio studied people with damage to the part of the brain where emotions are generated, he found that while they were unable to feel emotion as could have been expected, they also had something else in common: they couldn't make decisions.

They could describe what they should be doing in logical terms, but they found it very difficult to make even simple decisions, such as what to eat. Many decisions have pros and cons on both sides that make a rational decision about which is better difficult. And with no rational way to decide, these test subjects were unable to arrive at a decision. In his well-known book, *Descartes' Error*, Damasio argues that it is wrong to believe that we only think with our minds. He emphasized that our entire body and our emotions also have a key role in the way we think and in decision-making: 'the body... contributes a content that is part and parcel of the workings of the normal mind, [therefore] the mind is embodied, in the full sense of the term, not just embrained' (Damasio, 1994).

Damasio's theory stresses the crucial role emotion and feeling has in making every personal decision throughout our lives. He named the signals that guide us in our decision 'somatic markers' – gut feelings. By listening to your gut reactions, you can eliminate some negative alternatives immediately and choose from among fewer options. This use of emotion and gut feelings in decision making extends even to decisions we believe are logical. At the point of decision, our brain bases its fundamental decisions on two questions:

1 Have I seen this (or something similar) before? – Looking for a pattern.

2 Was it a good or bad experience? – Accessing an emotional memory.

If I have seen it before (or something similar) and it was a good experience, the result is a very strong thumbs-up to go ahead. As humans, we perceive this almost instantaneous process as intuition. When the basic gut feeling decision is made, with the help of the limbic systems that produce the somatic markers, other parts of the brain become involved to help explain and communicate the decision. These include the ventromedial prefrontal cortex and the medial orbitofrontal cortex: parts connected with valuation, predicted and experienced values (Figure 4.1).

These frontal lobes store a lot of interesting information, such as morals and values, including the genuine personal value that comes from the decision itself. They also hold future scenarios, trends and the correct, updated vocabulary. All this is needed for us to articulate the decision well and portray ourselves as serious and well-informed when we announce our decision or suggestion (Damasio, 1994).

Figure 4.1 Branding pattern recognition

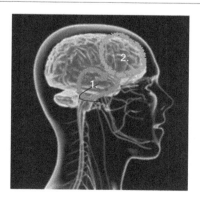

Key: 1. Limbic systems etc 2. Frontal cortex

Mirror neurons copy behaviour and read minds

Copying and becoming influenced by other people's behaviour, non-verbally, is an important part of relation branding. In this, we can make use of studies of mirror neurons. These mirror neurons respond in exactly the same way when we witness someone else performing an action as they do when we perform that action ourselves.

Mirror neurons were first discovered in the early 1990s, when a team of Italian researchers found individual neurons in the brains of macaque monkeys that fired both when the monkeys grabbed an object and when the monkeys watched another primate grab the same object. Giacomo Rizzolatti, the neuroscientist who with his colleagues at the University of Parma first identified mirror neurons, believes that the neurons could help explain how we 'read' other people's minds and feel empathy for them (Ferrari *et al*, 2003).

This inbuilt mirroring of actions that we see with actions that we do brings home the importance of one method of launching a new brand and business: using existing customers as a reference and sales force. One example of an amazing launch, achieved very quickly and very cheaply, is the marketing of Dropbox.

The Dropbox example of immediate gains

Founded in 2007 by MIT students Drew Houston and Arash Ferdowsi, Dropbox did no advertising at all. By relying only on existing customers to attract new ones, Dropbox still succeeded in become one of the leading cloud storage providers. But there were other businesses offering the same services. What made Dropbox so much more successful than others who had been in business for years? It was a simple idea: instant reward. It is hardwired into our brains to overvalue immediate gains, and overlook what we may gain in the future (Cohen, 2005).

This is why making a referring customer wait for their reward often fails. Most companies that try to use customers as a reference or sales force make the mistake of delaying the reward until the referred potential customer becomes a registered customer. Companies want to achieve the benefit before giving the reward. Dropbox, however, rewarded their customers immediately, as soon as they received the name and an e-mail address of a potential new customer.

It was not a huge reward – only 500Mb of storage, the smallest service Dropbox provided – but size is not important when you give an instant reward. The result is, of course, that you get a lot of names of new potential customers. And sooner rather than later, you will get business from this bulk. In Dropbox's case, this is exactly what happened. By being generous, they had more responses and were able to quickly build up their business. In general, people are more careful about giving a name than most companies think. This is why references from other customers and users matter so much. And the new brain research shows us how very important references are when you introduce something new to the market.

Another benefit of getting customers to refer friends is that it generates a behaviour pattern. Remember, the decision-making brain is not impressed with verbal recommendation, but it does notice behaviour. The friends we communicate with regularly generate very strong support for our decision making. We study, pick up new behavioural patterns from and gain inspiration from these friends. All this makes customer referral – word of mouth – one of the most important factors to consider when launching a new brand.

Are we genetically coded to make wrong decisions?

It's not only neurologists that make us aware of how irrational, and sometimes biased, our decision making is. Daniel Kahneman was one of two recipients of the Nobel Prize for Economic Sciences in 2002 for challenging assumptions on human rationality in economic theory.

Kahneman is known for his 2011 bestselling book, *Thinking, Fast and Slow*, and for developing the notion of the 'focusing illusion' with David Schkade, (Kahneman and Schkade 1998; Kahneman et al 2006). This theory helps to explain why people make mistakes when they estimate the effects different events will have on their futures, also known as affective forecasting. The illusion is created when people focus on the impact that one specific factor will have on their overall happiness. Often, people exaggerate the importance of this factor, and overlook many other factors with a far greater impact.

A similar psychological effect that affects people's judgement is anchoring. Here, the tendency is to make decisions after placing too high an emphasis on the first piece of information (the 'anchor'). This anchor, once set, allows and encourages judgements to be made by referencing the anchor, and it influences interpretations of other information (Kahneman and Tversky 1974). One example of this is setting a high initial price on a product. This sets the standard and makes any lower prices seem like good value, even if the price is still more than the product is really worth.

'Reality distortion field' or reframing?

When Steve Jobs met Robert Friedland in 1972, Robert was the spiritual-seeking proprietor of an apple farm commune. He introduced Steve Jobs to a principle called the 'reality distortion field'. In his 2011 biography Steve Jobs told his biographer, Walter Isaacson, 'Friedland... turned me on to a different level of consciousness' (Isaacson, 2011).

The 'reality distortion field' is an extreme version of what the psychologist Daniel Kahneman calls a 'pervasive optimistic bias' in his book: 'Most of us view the world as more benign than it really is, our own attributes as more favourable than they truly are, and the goals we adopt as more achievable than they are likely to be' (Kahnemann, 2011).

By creating a 'reality distortion field' you reframe a problem in such a way that others are more likely to accept your way of thinking. Steve Jobs was very good at reframing issues, and as such he was able to encourage people to look at old problems from a new angle and gain new insights and approaches to help find a solution.

This distortion of reality and reframing the problem has been used many times in politics. Martin Luther King reframed the political battle for civil rights as a dream that could be realized. President Kennedy's call to put a man on the moon within a decade reframed the problem of the Cold War with the Soviets even as it captured the imagination of those who heard it. By reframing the problem, you give yourself the chance to bring about major changes in the way people think (Kaipa, 2012).

The brand algorithm in the brain

In his book, *Branding with Brains: The science of getting customers to choose your company* (Walvis, 2010), Tjaco Walvis from the Netherlands formulated what he calls the 'algorithm in the brain' that makes the brand choices, in much the same way Google uses an algorithm to search the Web. This brain algorithm has three criteria that guide consumer choices of one brand over another. These are:

1 **Relevance.** The more distinctive and uniquely relevant a product or service is, the greater the chance it will be chosen by the customer. Relevant brands are better linked to the dopamine, or reward, system in the brain (part of the limbic systems), which strongly influences our behaviour.

2 **Coherence.** The more coordinated the branding efforts are over time and space, the greater the chance the brand will be chosen. Coherent branding means repeating the same message over the years and across all customer touch-points. This makes it easier for the brain to retrieve the brand and make it a winner in competition with others.

3 **Participation.** The more interactive the branding environment created for customers is, the more likely it is that the brand will be selected by the brain's algorithm. The brain forms numerous new cell connections in response to interactive environment, improving the memorability of a brand.

As an example, Tjaco Walvis notes that the Adidas brand's long-lasting campaign 'Impossible is nothing' demonstrates how all these factors come together to create an extraordinarily attractive and successful brand that many customers choose over competitors such as, for instance, Nike. He also shows these factors succeed in avoiding a number of traps. Distinctive relevance avoids the 'identity loss trap', coherence avoids the 'authenticity trap' and participation avoids the 'brand dilution trap' (Walvis, 2010).

Conclusion: Managing non-conscious customer minds

We are just in the infancy of what neurological research and modern up-dated psychology can do for a better customer experience brand outcome. The interest in the brain, and how people use their brains to make decisions between different brands, is not new. Obviously, it has always been a very attractive goal for any marketer to be able to go beyond the surface, deeper into people's minds, to find the secret of preferences and brand choices.

Now that new technology is giving us a map of the processes in our brains, we can turn this knowledge into a toolbox for today's brand builders. Within this new toolbox, we have access to an ability to focus on the dominant, non-conscious brain that is stimulated by patterns rather than details. We have access to the knowledge that the brain is always looking for the new and the unexpected – a tool we can use to create surprises that satisfy this craving and ensure our brand stands out from those of our competitors who don't use this tool. Through studying innovative people like Steve Jobs, we can see the powerful ability 'reality distortion fields' can have in changing people's mind-sets by reframing a problem (or possibility) in a new way.

Noble prize winners have helped show us how we can use the opportunity of securing initial information as a mental anchor in people's decision-making. We know how the whole body and the least intellectual parts of the brain (the limbic systems) are more important for decisions than the more intellectual part of the brain (the neo-cortex). And how mirror neurons allow us to read other people's minds, change feelings or introducing new behaviour without using one single word of communication, not least in the areas of involvement, participation and the increasing of visual social networking. This new knowledge of the brain shows us a reason to do things differently.

Still, until recently the general approach has remained quite rational and based on the idea that consumers make conscious and deliberate decisions and brand choices. It has been assumed that choices are based more on the functionality of the branded products, rather than their social, mental or spiritual dimensions. We now know that the functionality of the products is less important for branding than the social, mental or spiritual brand dimensions. This has led to a move away from the idea that consumer decisions are rational, and that branding is the same as advertising.

References

Berns, G, McClure, SM, Pagnoni, G and Montague, PR (2001) 'Predictability modulates human brain response to reward' [Online] Available from www.ncbi.nlm.nih.gov/pubmed [Last accessed 29.1.16]

Cohen, JD (2005) The vulcanization of the human brain: A neural perspective on interactions between cognition and emotion, *Journal of Economic Perspectives*, **19** (4), pp 3–24

Damasio, A (1994) *Descartes' Error: Emotion, reason, and the human brain*, Avon Books, New York

Dijksterhuis, A, Bongers, KCA, Bos, MW, van der Leij, A (2009) 'The rational unconscious: Conscious versus unconscious thought in complex consumer choice' [Online] www.econbiz.de/ [Last accessed: 15.2.16]

Ferrari, PF, Gallese, V, Rizzolatti, G and Fogassi L (2003) Mirror neurons responding to the observation of ingestive and communicative mouth actions in the monkey ventral premotor cortex, *European Journal Neuroscience*, **17** (8), pp 1703–1714.

Gilbert, D (2006) *Stumbling on Happiness*, Knopf, New York

Hawkins, J (2004) *On Intelligence*, Times Books, New York

Isaacson, W (2011) *Steve Jobs*, Simon and Schuster, New York

Kahneman, D (1998) Does living in California make people happy? A focusing illusion in judgments of life satisfaction, *Psychological Science*, **9**, pp 340–346

Kahneman, D (2011) *Thinking, Fast and Slow*, Farrar Straus & Giroux, New York

Kahneman, D and Schakade, DA (1998) Does living in California make people happy? A focusing illusion in judgments of life satisfaction, *Psychological Science*, **9** (5), pp 340–346

Kahneman, D and Tversky, A (1974) Judgment under uncertainty: Heuristics and biases, *Science*, **185**, pp 1124–1131

Kahneman, D, Kruger, AB, Schkade, D, Schwarz, N and Stone, AA (2006) Would you be happier if you were richer? A focusing illusion, *Science*, **312**, pp. 1908–1910

Kaipa, P (2012) Steve Jobs and the art of mental model innovation, *Ivy Business Journal* [Online] http://iveybusinessjournal.com/publication/steve-jobs-and-the-art-of-mental-model-innovation/ [Last accessed 4.4.16]

Schafe, GE, Nader, K, Blair, HT and LeDoux, JE (2001) Memory consolidation of Pavlovian fear conditioning: A cellular and molecular perspective [Online] www.ncbi.nlm.nih.gov/pubmed [Last accessed 29.1.16]

Walvis, T (2010) *Branding with Brains: The science of getting customers to choose your company*, FT Press, Harlow

Weinschenk, S (2011) *100 Things Every Designer Needs To Know About People*, New Riders, Berkeley

Context innovation

Surprise by reading the minds of customers and users

GoPro is a very interesting example of a true surprise brand from the very start. How can you create a multi-billion-dollar camera business in a world where everyone has a smartphone with a good camera in their pockets, and usually another camera in their household, too? Nick Woodman succeeded. He started his business in 2002, and has gone from sleeping out of his 1971 Volkswagen Bus and selling 35mm film cameras, to being the leading, fastest-growing camera company in the USA.

He is now a multi-billionaire, but his initial idea, in 2001, was simply a wrist strap that tethered already-existing cameras to surfers. After testing his first makeshift models on a surfing trip to Australia and Indonesia, he realized he would have to manufacture the camera, its housing and the strap together.

A decade later, GoPro had the highest-selling point-of-view camera on the market. Unlike the first version, which was a 35mm camera, the company's later products shoot panoramic, high-definition video that has become the standard in capturing action sports. Few skiers, snowboarders, divers, flyers or extreme sports enthusiasts can live without the images that come out of the GoPro. In the first half of 2012, GoPro was responsible for 21.5 per cent of all digital camcorder shipments in the USA and a third of the pocket camcorder market (Mac, 2013).

The company has an aggressive context-based marketing and social media strategy, as well as constant consumer-based technology advancements. It was in the right place at the right time. GoPro took advantage of a period when smartphones were making traditional digital cameras and camcorders obsolete.

In an interview with *Forbes*, Woodman pointed out that 'Consumers are no longer spending their money on point-and-shoot cameras – pocket cameras – because they already have that in the form of their smartphone. So they have disposable income for something like a GoPro, which is highly differentiated from a smartphone' (*Forbes*, 2013).

While sceptics are unsure of whether smartphones can stay out of GoPro's territory, Woodman says that the two devices are built to coexist, especially as his company builds out its Wi-Fi capabilities and smartphone applications. Woodman's vision is to build solutions that 'help people capture meaningful life's [sic] experiences in an engaging, immersive way' (*Forbes*, 2013).

And the likelihood that he is right is strengthened by the fact that today's iPhone users are getting so very used to always taking photos, including selfies, in whatever situation they are in. GoPro is simply extending the situations in which you can do this, without damaging your iPhone. GoPro has also become a cult item, a must-have for the adventurer. It is a way to share excitement with peers and admiring friends who are amazed, and wouldn't even dream of doing it themselves.

GoPro will most likely keep on surprising camera users all over the world. Doing this as a brand very much depends on quality users' experiences and context relevance. Go Pro is a typical outside-in type of branding. It began with the needs of a specific category of users – surfers – and ends with a life experience device for people who enjoy all kinds of outdoor activities, including skydiving, flying, golfing, hiking, snorkelling, skiing, hunting, racing, rafting and more. With GoPro, the word hero was given a new meaning as the name of one of its products. And any activity that could make you feel like a hero could now be captured on film. All these heroes participate by putting their images and videos on the Web; the best marketing a brand can get.

And maybe that is GoPro's most differentiating feature. The participation of customers and users builds up the brand and does most of the marketing. GoPro took advantage of customer involvement to create the brand and keep it going.

Brand context innovation

When the iPhone was introduced in 2007 and became a game changer in the smart mobile phones category, it did not typically invent a technology from scratch. Touch-screen technology already existed, but it hadn't been used properly. By employing the existing technology in a better, more entertaining, experience-oriented and playful way, it tuned into something that already existed in the consumers' minds. It realized something that was already envisioned and anticipated: the ability to not just directly control functions by moving fingers over a larger window that was used for many functions, but also to display the image and content larger, clearer and in a manner that made its use more flexible.

The iPhone was unique in its context, but it is still just one of many examples of the success that occurs when a brand and its products tune perfectly into the context of the user.

This is what I call 'brand context innovation'. Here, the innovation process doesn't start with the entrepreneur inventing something and then trying to get someone to like it and buy it, while fantasising about all the possible needs. On the contrary, context innovation starts from classic branding and innovation research: finding the true needs and great passions of a group of users. What works well for them, later proves to work well for other groups with different lives but parallel contexts. This why I love crowdfunding; it is the ultimate test of a product among passionate people, who like something so much they are willing not only to buy it, but also to invest in it.

Context first, then product

As I have said, for many years I taught and practiced the opposite: business strategy first, including the product idea or service concept, followed by brand strategy. I previously perceived the brand strategy as a subordinated support strategy, but later realized I had been looking at it in a traditional, marketing-centred way, in which the role of the brand is simply a way of packaging and selling the product. This is pure transaction branding, with the value proposition and brand story included in the brand strategy. In practice, all this went completely against my experiences and discoveries that branding and the brand is in fact the business strategy and the key to innovation.

The reason I finally woke up and changed my rhetoric was that I had seen (and participated in) too many unsuccessful ventures that either pivoted into something unplanned or were simply lucky enough to find success in something else. In most cases, though, they were not at all successful. Instead, the venture failed totally and silently, disappearing from the radar of innovations. There are of course many reasons for ventures to fail, but not addressing the relevant and real needs of potential users or customers is certainly the main one. If something sells well, a lot of other problems in a business become much easier to fix.

This insight is based on many years' experience building relation brands, and following the dramatic changes in the nature of branding because of the development of the internet. I have seen so many brands become successful not through what their founders planned and pushed on users but through pivoting in a new direction and serving actual needs in peoples' lives and minds. Through this unexpected and different turn, far from the original idea, brands can become hugely successful.

All this has led me to the point of insight where I feel I can no longer play along with an obsolete view of branding, but have instead to stand up for what could become successes in this new relationship-driven world. Playing with the forces, not against them; I simply had to break the mould.

Why is it essential to get into people's minds first?

I realized that everything has to start with whatever is troubling people, irritating them. Things that should be changed, that are waiting to be taken care of. Things that will be lost if not preserved. Things that need to be turned around to become something new or different. Very often the change, re-invention, fix or preservation is inspired by something in another part of life that has already changed. When things need to be taken care of, but no one has been able to do that before, we have the great *surprise effect* of brand context innovation, and the question in everyone's mind: why hasn't this been done before?

Sometimes these changes haven't been made because the technology hasn't been there. Technology is usually the driver of large-scale change. Technology, directly and indirectly, is always changing culture and behaviour, and these social and cultural changes then drive other changes in our lives. On a mega-level, we now know that digital technology and the internet have changed so much in our modern lives that we can talk about total change without exaggerating. Technology has changed our behaviour and our relationships with people, and these in turn dramatically drive change in all life and business contexts.

If we recognize a product, service, idea or experience, or find it similar to something we do recognize, and have a positive experience, we are likely to pick it up, buy it and use it. Equally important is recognising a solution to an irritation in our lives. The likelihood that we buy such a solution is huge, even without testing it. Merely identifying with the problem can sometimes be strong enough if it seems that the problem can finally be fixed.

Our traditional innovation system

Traditionally, our focus and belief system have, in an incredible way, promoted innovation. Innovations driven by the technology-inspired ideas of the entrepreneur can be perceived as a success long before any serious study is made of customer experiences, needs, preferences, aspirations or ideas.

This lack of respect for customer needs, for understanding their worlds or contexts, explains the failure of so many potential ventures and the waste of so much money and human energy. Recent research from Shikhar Ghosh shows that only one in four venture-backed start-ups succeed in providing a return of the venture capitalists' investments. In fact, according to Ghosh's research, if the definition of failure is extended to failing to reach a specified revenue growth rate or break by a specific date, the failure rate increases to more than 95 per cent of all start-ups (Gadge, 2012).

How to develop brand context innovation

My approach to creating a disrupter or a game-changer in any category of products or services is to focus on creating products tailored to existing user needs in real user contexts.

Let's look at an example of how to create a new innovative context brand in the marketspace of digital tablet devices.

1 **Discover the different user contexts.** We first need to find out, explore and create relationships with the different user contexts that already exist. In our example of digital tablet devices we already know some typical contexts for professionals and consumers, and we know some of the usage needs in different professions, like pilots. But we also see a need in service areas like checking-in and taking orders while on the move, instead of behind a desk. We notice that a lot of consumers use tablets and iPads to control different functions in their homes. A lot of brands have been successful in this space – Sonos and Nest come to mind with their home automation systems. So, we continue to look around and notice existing user contexts.

2 **Tap into the minds of users.** The next step is meeting individuals who represent user contexts that could be interesting, retrieving weak signals and using pattern recognition to find user patterns, clusters and insights. We can then use these insights to help us to formulate one or more winning contextual concepts for tablets. Here, we use an anthropological/ethnographic research approach that involves watching, and lightly leading

the people we interview towards the context space we want to investigate. We need to be sensitive to their free associations and listen to any weak signals that can lead to the discovery of unexploited underlying needs. We are looking for findings in users' minds that our competitors have not yet consciously accessed. We are looking for expressions of needs that are not yet publicly articulated.

3 **Design the product or service.** We then need to match existing tablet design technology to defined, detailed user contexts and create different, hypothetical tablet versions. What follows is, of course, building prototypes and creating branding for the selected tablet user contexts, including product names and both physical and UX (user experience) design. Finally, we return to the users, testing the concepts on them and modifying as needed.

This process is, of course, modelled on successful technology businesses like GoPro: finding contexts in which the product is used in different ways, solving different problems and meeting different needs, integrated with specific lifestyle and user situations. In the GoPro case study, the protected HD-cameras for surfing, skydiving, flying, skiing, scuba diving, sailing and more, created a new business and a new brand.

In the case of our tablets, it maybe something similar, but it can also be a very different UX on a different, tailored app, or a combination of something physical and something virtual. The latter is the approach of Parrot's Bepop AR Drone 3.0, which attaches a tablet to special handles that have functions and connections to other products – the drone itself and the Occulus Rift 3D headset. It also includes an updated, advanced, special app for the new quadcopter drone with its HD camera and extended operation distance.

These examples display the structure needed to face the challenge of creating brand context innovation.

Conclusion: Context innovation and using framing as a tool is key to successful customer experience branding

Most of the really powerful innovations that having an impact on customer experience branding have originated as context innovation developed through using framing as a tool. It can also be amazingly successful to apply this to branding innovations, by disrupting a traditional pattern of thinking and introducing a new framing.

Re-framing problems takes effort, attention, and practice, yet it allows you to see the world around you in a new light. You can practise reframing by physically or mentally changing your point of view, by seeing the world from others' perspectives, and by asking questions that begin with 'why'. Together, these approaches enhance your ability to generate imaginative, creative, innovative responses to the branding challenges that come your way.

References

Mac, R (2013) The mad billionaire behind GoPro: The world's hottest camera company, *Forbes*, 4 (3) [Online] www.forbes.com/ [Last accessed 29.1.16]

Forbes (2013) How GoPro made a billionaire [Online video] www.forbes.com/ [Last accessed 29.1.16]

Gage, D (2012) The venture capital secret: 3 out of 4 start-ups fail, *Wall Street Journal*, 20 September [Online] www.wsj.com/ [Last accessed 29.1.16]

Four-dimensional branding

Stretching the brand mind space for the unexpected

I first developed the idea of four-dimensional (4D) branding in 2000, and it became the book *4D Branding: Cracking the corporate code of the network society*. My purpose was to show that successfully differentiating branding in a new network-driven paradigm was no longer a matter of just the functional dimension. The functional dimension focuses on the product or service and its qualities, performance, design, packaging, ingredients, manufacturing techniques or methodologies. 4D branding includes this, but the focus is more and more on the other three brand dimensions: the social dimension, the mental dimension and the spiritual dimension.

The social dimension puts the brand in a social context. It integrates the brand into social groupings as an identity reference that includes name-dropping and status. The mental dimension plays on the individualized interpretations of the brand. Brands will always be perceived by individuals, and each individual will bring their own interpretation and meaning to the brand; Nike's 'Just do it' holds a different, personal significance for each individual.

Finally, the spiritual dimension deals with the big picture. It has less to do with religion, and more to do with the impact the brand, its products and its services have on society, the environment, the climate and human development. Positively participating in and contributing to these globally critical themes is an issue for mankind and in your business, taking what is now called corporate social responsibility (CSR) has also become critical. In short, the spiritual dimension deals with purpose and meaning.

The brand mind space

We can use this model (Figure 6.1) to see how successful brands have differentiated themselves by using all four dimensions. They 'stretch out' what I call the brand mind space: the space that a brand occupies in people's minds. I visualize this brand mind space as one of those slimes that kids play with. You can stretch them out nearly as far as you like and, when you let go, they retract to their original size and shape. I see a brand in much the same fashion; you have to stretch it out in the four dimensions to let it take space in people's minds.

Figure 6.1 The 4-D brand mind space model

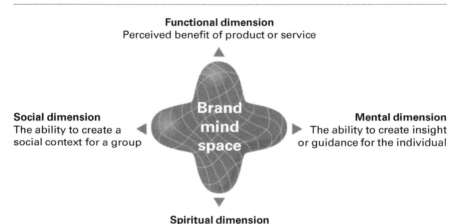

Functional dimension
Perceived benefit of product or service

Social dimension
The ability to create a
social context for a group

Brand mind space

Mental dimension
The ability to create insight
or guidance for the individual

Spiritual dimension
Perception of having a higher purpose or meaning in your industry,
and in the society: better quality of life for people, and for the planet

We can take a deeper look at these four dimensions and put them in context with the development of branding. Since the key reason for branding, historically, was to create demand in order to sell the products, this type of branding almost always promoted the unique benefits of the products; the so-called unique selling proposition (USP).

In 1961 Rosser Reeves made this statement in *Reality in Advertising*:

1 Each advertisement must make a proposition to the consumer. Not just words, not just product puffery, not just show-window advertising. Each advertisement must say to each reader: 'Buy this product and you will get this specific benefit'.

2 The proposition must be one that the competition either cannot, or does not, offer. It must be unique – either a uniqueness of the brand, or a claim not otherwise made in that particular field of advertising.

3 The proposition must be so strong that it can move the mass millions, ie pull over new customers to your product.

(Reeves, 1961)

This is exactly what I call the functional dimension, or the product dimension, of the brand. And when a product really is different and better, highlighting the USP works very well. But today, when we have a hard time finding a product that is uniquely different, we obviously need another branding idea. The dilemma of similarity is very well described in the book *Funky Business* by Kjell Nordström and Jonas Ridderstråle:

> The surplus society has a surplus of similar companies, employing similar people, with similar educational backgrounds, working in similar jobs, coming up with similar ideas, producing similar things, with similar prices, warranties and qualities.

(Nordström and Ridderstråle, 2000)

Something had to be done to fight this. As early as 1955 David Ogilvy, the grandfather of modern advertising, had a radical idea and introduced the concept of brand image. He believed that 'every advertisement must be considered as a contribution to the complex symbol, which is the brand image'.

Thus, I call this kind of brand building the social dimension in my 4D branding model. It is very much about the social brand image, the perception of the brand within a group of likeminded people. In this dimension, status and image are the essential drivers.

The opposite and complement to the social dimension is the mental dimension, or the individual dimension. This is the individual's relationship with the brand. It takes advantage of the fact that all brands are perceived individually, and are thus never exactly the same to any two individuals. Since our society is becoming more individualized in so many ways, triggering the creation of individualized personal brand perception is of growing importance. Especially as relation brands tend be more intimate with customers, the individual response mechanism within the brand becomes ever more important. We will continue to explore this in greater detail in later chapters.

The final dimension of the 4D branding model is the spiritual dimension, or the meaning dimension. This dimension addresses another important need that today's relation brands must fulfil in order to rise to their full potential. Brands must clearly take responsibility and participate in society. Through this, they fuel their relationships to matters that are important to people, more than just providing a quality functional product or service. It is important to place the brand in the big picture and use marketing to change the world for the better. Today, this responsibility is very relevant to any company.

Today, the 'big picture' very much includes the pressing global challenges; climate change and environmental issues, inequality and poverty, significant diseases (HIV/AIDS, cholera, malaria, cancer), unethical production and trade, and violence and terrorism. I prefer to call this sustainability branding, and maybe it is just 'the tip of the iceberg', as John Grant writes in his book, *The Green Marketing Manifesto* (2007):

> We may be only the tip of the iceberg, but our job is important because what we do is so visible. We are where all of the development behind the scenes in business and governments meet people's lives. We are part of the reason why big corporations with responsibility built in, why product and service inventors, why cultural change campaigns and why new business (and non-business) models may thrive. We can fan the flames of public enthusiasm. Which is why more companies and politicians will rush into this space. Not just because it is the right thing to do. But because it is smart too.
>
> (Grant, 2007)

The political correctness that followed the discussions outlined above has lost a little of its attraction from a branding point of view. A brand, fundamentally, needs to differentiate itself from its competitors. However, as the earlier demonstrations of the spiritual dimension have become accepted by almost everyone, there is no longer much controversy (and consequently no potential differentiation) concerning the need for a better life on Earth. Environmental protection, climate change responsibility, ethical and responsible behaviour, fighting poverty and the big global diseases are things we all want to do, and all businesses have to contribute to them even though governments have to take the lead.

Instead, for differentiating the brand and also to get closer to genuine individual interests, we need other kinds of ideas to build the spiritual dimension. These issues are more personal, emotional and psychological. They are issues of general human concern that must be addressed in order to create a better world to live in. It becomes essentially about a better and 'deeper' quality of life.

The theme of changing the world is a very common one, and it is a driving force for most entrepreneurs. And not only does that goal drive their initial venture, but when they become successful and wealthy, entrepreneurs tend to maintain a great focus on 'fixing the world'. Their entrepreneurial, hands-on approach to correcting wrongs and making things better often uses new technology and new approaches to old problems.

Businesses in these digital, interactive, transparent times have great potential to release business ideas and initiatives by including these four dimensions in branding. By stretching out the brand mind space, you utilize a multidimensional approach in your brand, and thereby differentiate yourself against competitors. When you take up more space in people's minds, you can create a stronger relationship and deeper ties between the brand and the person.

And, you create more surprises to fuel your relation brand.

4D branding as a surprise generator

The 4D branding model and the brand mind space are effective not only in building a relation brand, they are also effective surprise generators. The 4D brand mind space is the ideal strategy tool when looking for surprises to fuel your brand relationships. The biggest problem when business people sit down and try to create positive surprises is that they are often one-dimensional.

Simplifying the process and remaining within product development and the functional dimension, for example, is a shame when there are plenty of opportunities to surprise in the other three dimensions. The functional dimension also has the disadvantage of being the easiest of the dimensions for your competitors to copy, if you are successful. Instead, by forcing yourself to look into the other three dimensions, you can find much more exciting differentiation. Real surprise follows a real disruption. If you can create effective surprises within the social, mental and spiritual dimensions as well, you strengthen your brand ties to your customers and users immeasurably, as we will see in the next chapter.

The 4D surprise creation tool

As you develop your branding and your systematic approach to creating surprise, it is important to understand that the more you can target your products and services to meet specific needs, the more successful your marketing will be. People like to be surprised that you are satisfying their needs – and their silent expectations.

A successful new business or start-up is usually perceived as disruptive, and the mechanism of disruption is there to challenge expectations. First, you have to be sure about existing customer needs and connected expectations. Then, the expectations must be challenged enough to create a perception of disruption. This is measured in the amount of surprise: the 'wow' effect.

With this surprise index (Figures 6.2 and 6.3) you can evaluate whether your start-up has enough disruptive surprise power to become successful in people's minds and in the market place. The surprise index also becomes an amazing tool for systematically creating surprises.

The 4D brand mind space is the backbone of the surprise index, and you can use the same four dimensions to help develop successful surprises. A tour of the index can begin wherever you like. Traditionally, most business have started (and unfortunately remained) with the functional surprise. It was the only dimension the old transaction brand world considered.

Of course, any brand needs to produce a new product once in a while, but a wider view of what a product is makes it interesting to look at the social surprise for inspiration. How can you, in a surprising way, introduce a networking idea as a new brand product or concept? Apple did this with iStore and Apple Pay, and now with Apple Music. Socially connecting different parts of your business category can create something that feels new and fresh, a disruptive, surprising initiative.

Figure 6.2 The surprise index: using the brand mind space model to help surprise exceed expectation

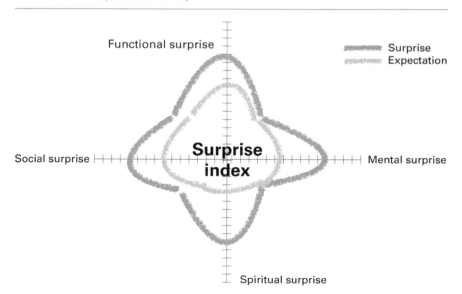

Figure 6.3 The surprise generator: measuring surprise on the surprise index

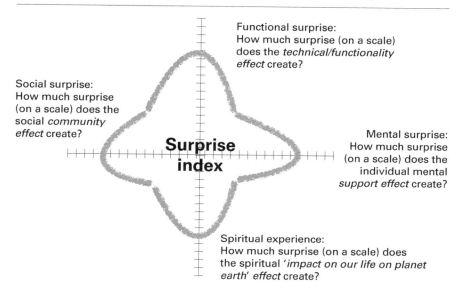

Or, why not exploit the mental surprise. Here, it is about individual customer experiences and relationships with the brand. Uber, with its individual perception, is a good example of this, being first surprising and then joyful again and again.

Last, but not least, is the spiritual surprise that addresses the big change. Consider the disruption potential in your business or category by thinking big and attempting to increase the quality of life, right a wrong or prevent the end of something good.

Conclusion: The stretching out of the brand to create surprise

The idea of the brand being stretched out to take place in people's minds in the four dimensions is almost physical and dynamic. This stretching is a continuous process throughout the life of a brand and can be achieved by creating surprises in each of the dimensions. The surprise index can be used to effectively and systematically plan and continuously fashion new surprises.

Using the four dimensions as an inspiring tool helps to remind the managers of a brand to create surprises in all the dimensions, not only for variation, but also to cover all the important aspects of the brand. With the surprise index you can estimate the level of expectation the brand can achieve in each brand dimension and what level of surprise it will take to create a surprise effect relative to that expectation level. This is further detailed in the next chapter.

References

Reeves, R (1961) *Reality in Advertising*, Knopf, New York

Nordström, K and Ridderstråle, J (2000) *Funky Business: Talent makes capital dance*, Pearson Education, London

Ogilvy, D (1955) *The Image of the Brand: A new approach to creative operations* [Online] www.brandstrategygroup.de/texte/ogilvy_the-image-of-the-brand_1955.pdf [Last accessed 29.1.16]

Grant, J (2007) *The Green Marketing Manifesto*, Wiley, Chichester

The Easter egg effect

07

How to produce anticipated surprise

Every time we get a colourful, foil-wrapped Easter egg, we know what's inside, don't we? And yet, we still get surprised and excited when we remove the packaging and see what we anticipated. The same effect can be had from Christmas or birthday presents, even though we don't always know what they contain.

The verbal expressions of anticipation we express (usually loudly and boldly) vary according to the power the surprise-pattern has created in our emotional relation brains (the limbic systems). But the big question is, why are we surprised at all?

What is surprise, anyway?

Surprise is a short mental and physiological state. It is described as a startle-response that results from an unexpected event. Surprise can be positive or negative, or even neutral, depending on the situation. Both pleasant and unpleasant surprises can vary in intensity from a very mild reaction to a fight-or-flight response (Casti, 1994). We usually express surprise through our expressions and the following features:

- raised eyebrows, so they become curved and high;
- horizontal wrinkles across the forehead;
- wide-open eyes, often exposing the white of the eye around the iris;
- pupil dilation or pupil constriction;
- dropped jaw that parts the lips and teeth, with no tension around the mouth.

(Burgoon and Hale, 1988; Ellis, 1981; Ekman and Friesen, 1975)

However, spontaneous, involuntary surprise is often expressed for only a fraction of a second. What follows, almost immediately, may be joy, fear or confusion. While many associate the jaw dropping as a measure of the strength of the surprise, in some cases it may not drop at all. The most distinctive and universal sign of surprise is probably the raising of the eyebrows.

The theory about the effects of surprise

Understanding surprise is understanding humour. The essence of humour lies in two factors: the relevance factor and the surprise factor. To produce humour, or surprise, it is first necessary to present something familiar or relevant to the audience. Invoking the audience's familiarity by using this relevance factor enables them to believe they understand the situation and know the natural follow-through. The humour then comes from presenting a twist that the audience did not expect, or interpreting the situation in an unexpected way. These twists and unexpected interpretations create the surprise factor (Reizenzein et al., 2006; Kalat, 2009).

Surprise is connected to the idea of following a set of rules, or a behavioural pattern. When the events of reality do not follow these rules and patterns, the result is surprise. In this way, surprise can be seen as the difference between what we expect and what actually happens.

However, surprise does not always have to mean the violation of expectation or behaviour outside the expected range. The surprise that follows a communication can also be a confirmation of something we anticipated and wanted, or behaviour that lies within the expected range. In fact, positive, confirming, behaviour increases the level of attraction to the source of the surprise. Negative violations decrease the attraction. We much prefer to be the recipient of a surprise party than of a parking ticket. As brand managers, we want to harness the power of positive surprises to enhance credibility, power, attraction and persuasiveness. We also want to avoid negative surprises that may reduce these qualities.

Surprise is sometimes called the 'wow' effect, and it signals the outcome of 'disruption', a commonly discussed concept in business today. Many successful businesses have disrupted the prevailing pattern in their business area, and in many cases their success is based on this (Silva, 2009).

The deeper psychological effects of surprise

Surprise is a strong neurological alert that tells us something is important about this moment and that we have to pay attention. It hijacks our cognitive resources and pulls them into the moment. That can be uncomfortable for some people, but it is also exciting because your attention is completely in the moment. Being surprised causes humans to physically freeze for 1/25th of a second (Luna and Renninger, 2015). After which, the surprise usually triggers something in the brain. It's a moment that generates extreme curiosity in an attempt to figure out what is happening during a surprise.

What follows is a shift. The surprise can force you to change your perspective, to change the way you've been looking at things. This disruption effect is part of the surprise. It is what makes us think: 'I wasn't expecting someone to surprise me and now I've just had this pleasant experience, I have to change the way I think about this person, and maybe even our whole relationship'.

When we're surprised, for better or for worse, our emotions intensify by two, three, or even more, times. If we're surprised by something positive, we feel more intense feelings of happiness or joy than we would have without the surprise. And this intensity is what makes the positive impact on the relationship with the person, or brand, much more significant. This is, of course, why surprise is of such importance for today's relation brands.

Surprise in branding has two perspectives: embracing it and engineering it. You need to not only be looking at how you can create surprise, you also need to train your brain to be comfortable accepting surprise. By that I also mean being comfortable with uncertainty, ambiguity and change. These days, this surprise readiness skill has become an incredibly important skill for all of us. In our digital media world, it's more obvious that it is important to learn how to orchestrate or engineer surprises. It is easy to see how this is about getting people's attention and bringing them delight in order to make them curious and excited about what your brand has to offer.

Anticipation – the basis of surprise

We all know the feeling of waiting for something exciting to happen. It's a feeling that can consume your thoughts and fill your mind. Whether it's a personal celebration or the well-publicized product release of something you have been waiting for, seeing glimpses and hints of what is to come heightens desire and the eagerness to finally get it.

But it's not just anticipation that offers value that might not otherwise be there. If you also include scarcity, the effect is enhanced considerably. Some marketers are masters at combining anticipation and scarcity with promises that most people don't believe they would fall for. But promises paired with warnings, such as 'Sign up now, before it's too late...' and 'Only 500 spaces available!' are always alluring. This kind of anticipation, built up over time, draws out the competitive spirit that has always driven humans. The delay before satisfying the anticipation gives people time to fear they will not get what they are waiting for. This, in turn, increases the desire and the willingness to sacrifice time and money to ensure that they are first in line when the time comes.

Using anticipation to build your brand and increase your business can sometimes feel as though you are just manipulating your customers and users. But if you build your strategy on the business ethnography we discussed in Chapter 3, you will understand what your customers' and users' unmet, and sometimes unspoken, needs are. You then only need to follow through and promise to meet these needs in order to create value through anticipation. If your customers have been waiting for a desired feature or function, let them know it's on the way in the next release.

Used carefully, making sure you never promise something you can't deliver in a timely manner, anticipation can attract new customers, cement the loyalty of existing customers and expand on your brand value.

Half of customer happiness is surprise

When we think of happiness, and what generates it, we often look at the event that brought happiness in isolation. But the time leading up to the event, anticipating it, and the time after the event, remembering it, bring at least as much happiness as the event itself. Happiness is as much built of moments of anticipation and remembering as of doing. This is why companies and brands must keep the joy of anticipation, and memory, in mind if they are to deliver true happiness to their customers.

In fact Marsha Richins, a professor at the University of Missouri, found that consumers receive more pleasure during the anticipation phase of a purchase than during the acquisition phase (Richins, 2013). As brand owners, you can harness and maximize the pleasure of this anticipation phase, through teasing, tempting and treating your customers.

Just as the trailer of a long-awaited film gives people something to look forward to long before the experience begins, so must brands *tease* their customers with leaked information and hints of what is coming. By increasing your customers' exposure to your brand and your promised product or service, you can also *tempt* them with the unfamiliar and unexpected. The very act of exposure to the new and the different increases a person's favourability towards it (Zajonc, 2001).

You can also offer your brand as a *treat*, a reward to look forward to. This can be done through limited availability, like seasonal sweets and foods that people look forward to all year. Another successful approach is the one Audible chose, making your brand an everyday treat that people can enjoy at any time. The Amazon audio book company portrays everything from the daily commute to mundane chores as an opportunity to escape into the pleasure of your choice of audio book.

When the anticipation phase is over, and you begin the acquisition phase of a purchase, the best way to keep a customer happy, and increase that happiness, is through interaction. By intervening, and nudging the customer towards the happiest path you can enhance your customer experience and gain greater loyalty for your brand. But guiding your customers on the path that will give them most satisfaction can be tricky. People are easily distracted. An immersive entrance and clear, direct instructions and exits encourage customers along the right path.

After you have generated the joy of anticipation, and the pleasure of a satisfying customer experience, it is the memory of the experience that determines if the customer will return, or even tell their friends about your brand. The problem here is that memories are not perfect representations of our experiences. Therefore, getting memories on your side can be the key to customers coming back and bringing their friends along with them.

When Daniel Kahneman presented a talk at an official TED conference, he said that 'endings are very, very important' (Kahneman, 2010). The ending dominates a person's memory of events. The new Spring NYC shopping app demonstrates how to finish strong with a thank you e-mail from the CEO as well as a personalized, hand-written thank-you letter from a member of the Spring NYC team.

The memory phase is also a good time for fresh surprises. Unpredictable and surprising events are more likely to be remembered than expected moments. And each time you remind your customers of your brand, product or service, new memories are created. With your brand, always consider how you can remind your customers of the benefits you provide and reinforce your positive attributes.

Emotions matter with branding, and the way to creating a positive, happy customer experience lies through understanding what creates happiness: not just delivering what the customer expects, but also in the anticipation of that delivery and the memory of it. By expanding our view of customer experience to include the time before and after the sale, we open up new possibilities of experience innovation.

Start with needs, create trust and anticipation, then surprise with delivery

Following the path detailed above, you start devising your branding strategy by considering whom the market for your product or service is. And be generous with the boarders here; almost all categories have customers 'we didn't think of'. It's better to be wider and more generous than you imagine necessary. It is more 'expensive' to lose unexpected users, than it is to reach out to too many. In each communication, and in selecting the media audience, ask whom this is for. Is it for your existing customers or potential customers, your existing employees or potential employees, your old or new business partners?

Make promises you can keep and meet their anticipated needs. In order to create trust, you need to fulfil anticipations, and anticipations always go back to needs. However, as Maslow shows us in his hierarchy of needs, these needs are different for different people (Figure 7.1).

Figure 7.1 Maslow's hierarchy of needs

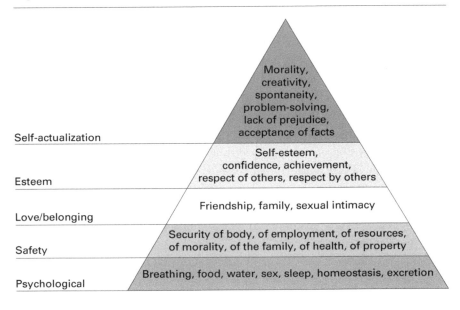

This hierarchy of needs applies in most decision situations. When you buy a car, for example, do you buy one for 'safety', one that all your friends have or like ('belonging'), or one that makes you feel good ('self-esteem')?

Just as you make buying decisions based on your underlying needs, so do your customers. But is there a need that dominates your market? Do more people in your target market want 'safety' over 'self-esteem'? Do more of them want a sense of 'love/belonging'? This is what you have to find out. And when you have, focus on delivering proof of trust and surprise by meeting anticipated needs.

The Easter egg effect

Obviously, in branding we are more interested in creating the positive and disrupting effects of surprise. Presenting the idea of systematic, positive surprise has become one of the most important tactical activities to successfully build a modern relation brand. Many people comment on the difficulty of producing a constant flow of surprises. There is also the issue of surprise fatigue.

First, let me address the difficulty many people have in producing a series of surprises, with the ambition of one major surprise a year for each brand. The truth is that if you focus on simply doing it, building a series of surprises is not that difficult at all. But we initially need to understand: what is the Easter egg effect?

I have come to the conclusion that there is a need within all humans for a) repetition of surprise and b) confirmation that our anticipations are correct and fulfilled. This is why surprise doesn't have to be a total surprise to be effective; it can equally well be the pure joy we express when our expectations are confirmed.

What, then, does this mean for the creators of continual surprises? One conclusion is that the surprise doesn't have to be fantastic to be exciting. And repetition is my answer to the question of fatigue: do we, at some point, get tired of surprises? I believe the answer is 'no, never'. This urge is deep within us, and within our human mental story. We never tire of surprise! Whether it's gifts for Christmas, or simply greetings on our birthdays, even people who officially say they don't want anything for their birthday are usually happy to get a surprising gift.

One very successful company that does this all the time is Apple. After the death of Steve Jobs, a well-loved and influential leader, every setback seemed to proclaim a crisis arisen as a result of his death, from the 'disappointing' iPhone 5 to the Apple Maps failures (Rushe, 2013). This perception of a crisis led to dissatisfaction among its customers, the loss of some employees, and a fall in their share price. It was two years before Apple launched something new, not just incremental version improvements of existing products. And when Tim Cook finally stood on stage to present one new product after the other, it was a long-anticipated event. Many people felt they already knew what would take place.

What was presented at this event put Apple back on track to being perceived as the innovation machine it had been under Steve Jobs. However, if you analyse the real surprise effect, it was not the products that were presented. The products and technologies that Apple 'introduced' had been discussed among Apple fans for at least a year and a half. In some cases Apple was, amazingly, the last to present these products. Some, like big screen smartphones and smart watches, had been on the market for several years. In fact, Apple's smart watch, launched in 2015, came 17 years after Steve Mann's Linux powered watch, the first watch that could communicate wirelessly with computers and other wireless-enabled devices.

We can see the whole event as a typical Easter egg effect. Surprise does not have to be all that surprising to become a surprise. Confirming speculations and delivering on anticipations is sometimes enough. You don't have to be uniquely and absolutely first. If the brand has the strength and self-confidence to create big expectations, that can be enough. And as always, the real surprise-confirming surprise came later, when Apple sold these items very well, better than competitors with the same technology – something that was initially doubted by experts.

Conclusion: The power of anticipation and surprise

The concepts of anticipation and surprise are fundamental to modern relation branding. They are the driving forces that allow successful relation brands to exist. Understanding these concepts, and how you can use them to create customer happiness before, during and after your interaction with your customers, can boost your brand both financially and in the minds of customers and potential customers. Anticipation, and confirming anticipation, generates the Easter egg effect, which can generate a chain of surprises to keep your customers happy and loyal. For this reason, brand managers need to create a foundation that facilitates engineering surprise from the beginning, with a code and motto designed to guide the brand into the future.

References

Burgoon, JK and Hale, JL (1988) Nonverbal expectancy violations: Model elaboration and application to immediacy behaviors, *Communication Monographs*, 55, pp 58–79.

Casti, J (1994) *Complexification: Explaining a paradoxical world through the science of surprise*, HarperCollins, New York

Ekman, P and Friesen, WV (1975) *Unmasking the face*, Prentice Hall, Inc, Englewood Cliffs

Ellis, CJ (1981) The pupillary light reflex in normal subjects, *British Journal of Ophthalmology*, 65 (11), pp 754–759 (November)

Kahneman, D (2010) The riddle of experience vs. memory. [Online video] www.ted.com/talks/daniel_kahneman_the_riddle_of_experience_vs_memory [Last accessed 29.1.16]

Kalat, JW (2009) *Biological Psychology*, 10th edn, Cengage Learning, Andover

Luna, T and Renninger, L (2015) *Surprise: Embrace the unpredictable and engineer the unexpected*, Perigee Books, New York

Reisenzein, R, Bördgen, S, Holtbernd, T and Matz, D (2006) Evidence for strong dissociation between emotion and facial displays: The case of surprise, *Journal of Personality and Social Psychology*, 91 (2), pp 295–315 (August)

Richins, M (2013) When wanting is better than having: Materialism, transformation expectations, and product-evoked emotions in the purchase process, *Journal of Consumer Research*, 40 (1), pp 1–18 (June)

Rushe, D (2013) Apple earnings expected to disappoint after iPhone 5C gamble falls flat, *Guardian*, 28 October [Online] www.theguardian.com/ [Last accessed 29.1.16]

Silva, PJ (2009) Looking past pleasure: Anger, confusion, disgust, pride, surprise, and other unusual aesthetic emotions, *Psychology of Aesthetics, Creativity, and the Arts*, 3 (1), pp 48–51 (February)

Zajonc, RB (2001) Mere exposure: A gateway to the subliminal, *Current Directions in Psychological Science*, 10 (6), pp 224–228 (December)

Coding for surprise

08

The brand code and motto

The brand code encapsulates the future positioning of the brand. It answers the question: what should this company really be about? It involves working through a series of possible scenarios to gain an understanding of how the brand might appeal to its various audiences. The brand code is the character that the brand plays on the stage. It is not the actor; it is the role the actor has to play. The actors can be anyone from a salesperson to a receptionist to the art director at an advertising agency. The actor's job is to interpret the role and the character and bring them to life, making them convincing and believable.

Needless to say, many interpretations are possible and also encouraged. In order to effectively utilize the creativity and personal talents of your people, it is important to give them a great deal of freedom in interpreting the brand code. But at the same time, in order to keep the brand consistent and homogeneous for the audience, it's important to ensure that the brand code is precise and well defined. The brand motto facilitates both of these conflicting needs by defining the core principle that the whole of the brand code is built on.

The purpose of the brand code is to create a future-driven brand. The brand code extracts your company's DNA code, or that for your product or service; everything else will be derived from or tuned into this code. It is the core of your company. It is an important instrument in all kinds of decision making; not only is it convenient in the decision process, allowing you always to back up your decisions by referencing the code, but it is also necessary in order to rapidly build a strong, well-defined and successful brand. The consistent branding approach that a brand-driven company takes to everything, on an everyday basis, is the most important secret of its success.

The brand code is a statement of what your company or your product stands for. It tells a story about your company. It is the business idea, the positioning, the vision, the mission and the values all in one package.

The brand code

The brand code model consists of, and is a synthesis of, six parts or backgrounds (Figure 8.1). The first three parts of the brand code are rooted in the brand's present situation in its marketplace. The other three parts are the 'tomorrow' aspects of the brand that drive the brand dynamically into the future.

The six parts are:

- product/benefit;
- positioning;
- style;
- mission/meaning;
- vision;
- values.

Together they create the brand code that is pulled into one expression by the brand motto that represents the core of the brand code.

Product/benefit

This section of the brand code is a carefully phrased description of the benefits the customer will experience through your company's deliverables: the product, service, knowledge, and so on. In most cases, this is an easy

Figure 8.1 The brand code model: brand code and brand motto

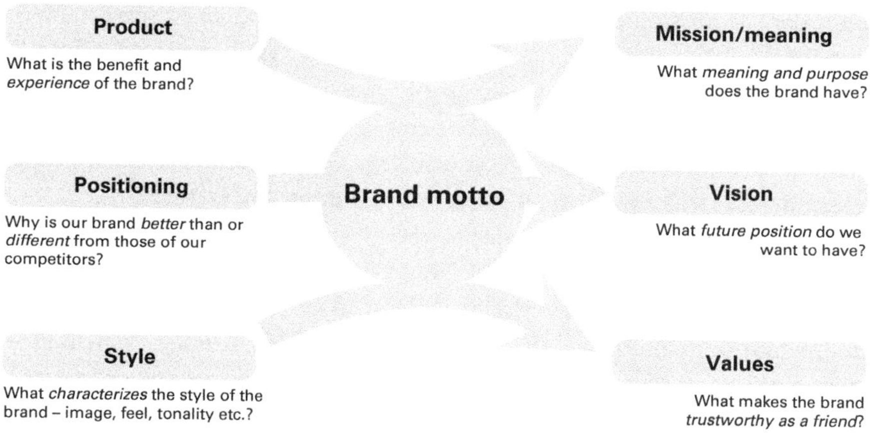

Product

What is the benefit and *experience* of the brand?

Mission/meaning

What *meaning and purpose* does the brand have?

Positioning

Why is our brand *better* than or *different* from those of our competitors?

Brand motto

Vision

What *future position* do we want to have?

Style

What *characterizes* the style of the brand – image, feel, tonality etc.?

Values

What makes the brand *trustworthy as a friend*?

task, but sometimes it takes a little work to go beyond the clichés of your business and find the bottom-line offer that you want to present to your customers. The benefit is closely related to the functional dimension we discussed in Chapter 6.

Positioning

This part of the brand code describes your response to the classic business positioning question: why are you better than and/or different from your competitors? Remember that the brand is the differentiation code of your company. Here, we begin to pin down our ability to create a difference. Usually this includes your competence, doing something very well for a specific target audience. You might also have competencies in your company that are not yet communicated in the benefit you deliver to your customers. The positioning element in the brand code also spins off the functional dimension.

Style

The last part of the brand code that is rooted in the current situation is style. Here, you describe the personal traits, image, attitude, and behaviour of the brand, whether that is the company or a product. Another name for this is personality. It is that part of personal appearance that immediately meets the eye. The style is heavily influenced by the social dimension.

Mission/meaning

When you begin to look forward into the future situation, you need to consider the mission or meaning of you company, product or service. Here, you need to go beyond the benefits to the customer and explore the brand's role in society. This does not necessarily mean the global society, but can remain tied to your local society. The perspective should be longer and wider than is traditionally the case when using the word mission. It has a deeper meaning, more like purpose; it is the 'why' and the 'big picture'.

For most companies that want to recruit young talent in a competitive market, this is a crucial part of the brand code. Young people in particular want a purposeful job, and this is at least as important as the monetary compensation. Companies that are not able to explain what contribution they make to society at large may not be on the shortlist of prospective workplaces for such people.

The mission and meaning are also very useful for directing public relations activities. They are strongly inspired by the spiritual dimension and the mission often turns the brand from a commercial brand into a stakeholder brand by giving the company the capacity for a higher pursuit.

Vision

The word vision has many definitions and is used in very different ways in management strategy. I use it in a very pragmatic way. Vision in the brand code is the positioning for the future: which market do we want to be in? And what role do we want to have in that market?

Quite often, you have to create your own market. A typical example of this is when Rollerblades created the market for inline skating. However, a common problem with creating a market that wasn't there before is that you risk becoming synonymous with the concept, rather than a distinct leading brand. When Rollerblades faced the prospect of becoming a general term for inline skates, they launched a marketing campaign to protect their name. You can compare this to the way the brands Xerox, Vespa, and Thermos have degraded and become generic terms.

The most successful brands have a clear vision for not only their future marketplace, but also what they want to provide, to whom and usually when. The timing is not a necessary part of the brand code, since it is difficult to determine and less important for determining how brand is perceived, but it is important in a business plan. Your vision is the most dynamic aspect of the brand code.

Values

The final aspect of the brand code you need to consider is the brand's values. I usually describe corporate values as rules of life. Sometimes, you meet people who live by very strong rules, and this is impressive no matter how peculiar these rules might be. Values emphasize the trustworthiness of the brand, as well as the long-term personality that guarantees continuity, just as values do in a personal friendship.

The keywords attached to your values are important and should be chosen with care, even though they are mainly non-verbal. A favourite word like honesty is easy to put in without commitment, but imagine a worst-case scenario for your business and ask how much you would, without hesitation, let it cost you to be honest – $50 million? $100 million? $200 million?

Important as it is to have an ethical ethos to drive your company, it can be dangerous if you are caught by journalists, customers, or competitors not living up to your own ethics. Take the personal values of your staff as the starting point. In entrepreneurial businesses, the values of the founder are usually set as corporate values. This makes them far more genuine than a contrived corporate strategy.

Working out values often leads to a discussion about whether a specific word is a value or a style. Customers can easily notice and identify a style, while it takes some time to experience a value. A value is a long-term feature, and someone might need to know your company or use your products or services for some time before they experience the values. Values are more philosophical in nature.

In addition to these six elements, I sometimes add two more. I look at *stakeholders* in order to clarify relationships between the brand and its various audiences and constituencies. I also examine *structure* in order to determine whether a brand is an ingredient brand or a master brand with several sub-brands.

The brand motto

The brand motto encompasses and summarizes the brand code. It can be a few key words or a short sentence. Sometimes it's tempting to use the brand code in your communication as a tag line or generic statement, like 'Connecting People' for Nokia. However, I usually recommend that my clients begin with using the brand code as the internal company mantra of the company; not used outside, but kept as a secret weapon to guide everybody in everyday situations.

Once you are satisfied with all your inputs, consider what would help you truly differentiate your company, product or service. In a few words, describe what would recreate your brand in someone's mind; synthesize all the elements. The more freely you think, the better. You might end up with more than one possibility, but you will almost certainly feel that one is stronger, that it might be the right motto.

Test your best idea against the six elements. If it connects with and is supported by at least two or three elements, then you'll be fine. Make sure you also check that it doesn't conflict with the rest of the elements and verify that you are able to use the brand code as a tool to drive your company forward. Can you use it to initiate an attitude and make decisions? Does your brand code contain a future drive? If the answers to these questions are yes, then you probably have the right brand code and motto. Give your brand code some time to establish itself; it often requires a couple of weeks.

Pick it up and look at it a few times during this period. The best brand code doesn't make people super-enthusiastic at first. The best ones grow with time, and grow your brand.

When a company already has a brand strategy, you can examine that strategy, de-code it and restructure it to fit this brand code format. The advantage to this is that it becomes much more obvious if there is something missing. Existing brand strategies do not usually contain everything that you need to fully complete the brand code model. In most cases, the missing aspect is the vision. This is because, in my experience, most company visions are not true visions of the future, but are merely a statement of what the company is doing today. This is not sufficient to guide your brand into the future and I recommend a vision workshop to solve that (see page 000).

My full branding process

To give you an idea how I work with my clients, this is the full Brandflight branding and customer experience process, which consists of 12 strategic and tangible activity deliverables.

1 **Understanding.** The process begins by understanding our client's business and exactly what the client expects the result of the branding and customer experience development process to be. This allows us to move towards the correct goal, and also to correct any misconceptions about what branding and customer experience is.

    Deliverable: Clients identify for themselves the need and reason for improving their brand and customer experience. This is an important insight for many customers.

2 **Modern branding and customer experience lecture.** Once we know what our clients expect we update our clients on the current situation and latest developments in branding, along with what is required for a modern brand to become successful. Due to the maturing force of the internet in all life and business functions, branding has undergone a fundamental change from transaction brands with a total focus on the product to relation brands, in which the brand is a relationship between the brand and the customer. The new relation brands can only be managed with a new kind of brand strategy.

    Deliverable: Clients understand how branding has changed in such a fundamental way, which enables them to correctly identify their own needs

▶

and reason for branding. Knowing how a modern brand is built and functions in people's minds, as well as internally in their own organisation and externally in society, is extremely inspiring for most clients. As such, this is a very valuable knowledge deliverable for future success.

3 **Brand vision workshop.** The first of several workshops in the brand strategy process covers defining the brand vision. Clients are encouraged to visualize their business and customer interaction 10 to 15 years in advance.

   Deliverable: One of the key success factors for any business and any brand is a clear vision in which the leadership of the business can see how they want to develop within a 10 to15 year perspective. Without a clear future destination/vision, it's impossible to successfully lead a business. This vision has to be formulated and communicated inside the company to become a priority strategy tool for the leadership.

4 **Brand mind space workshop.** The second workshop covers how the client wants the brand to be perceived. This is the desired result in the minds of customers and key stakeholders. The brand is mapped in the four dimensions: *functional* – the tangible pragmatic product, benefit or outcome of the brand; *social* – the social context of the brand and identification with the brand by groups of people; *mental* – the individual aspect of the brand, how individuals find/identify with the brand through features, deliverables, criteria, etc.; *spiritual* – the 'why' of the brand, its delivery on a higher level as part of a bigger picture in the life and society of human beings. Sometimes with existing brands we perform a lengthy individual interview research with customers (called business anthropology or business ethnography) with the result in these four dimensions.

   Deliverable: A high-level multi-dimensional insight into how the client imagines customer perception of their brand. This is an important target document for the new brand strategy.

5 **Brand positioning workshop.** In this third workshop we map out competitors relative to the client's brand, in a field defined by two axes with the client brand in the upper right corner. One axis is 'Best at...': the tangible, functional, product-like outcome. The other axis is 'Passionate about...': the more emotional, important and motivating aspect of the brand.

   Deliverable: A classical definition of how the brand is better than and different from the competitors' brands highlighting two important aspects, one rational and one more emotional.

6 **The brand code and motto.** Halfway through the process we create the main brand strategy document, and define the central outcome of the branding and customer experience. The brand code has six inputs: product/benefit, positioning, style, mission/meaning, vision and values.

Deliverable: With the brand code and motto, the client leadership has an excellent instrument to manage not only the marketing, but also decision making throughout the entire organisation, in all departments and for all functions.

7 **Brand activity generator.** This is the manifestation of the brand in tangible activities and communication (Figure 8.2).

Deliverable: We place the new brand code and motto in the middle and stretch out the brand with respect to activities that manifest the brand into the four dimensions of the brand mind space, corresponding to what we want the brand to become in people's minds.

8 **Brand story.** We use a special format of storytelling that we developed from movie scriptwriting to create a consistent and synchronized brand story.

Deliverable: This is a one-minute story that can be told over and again to all stakeholders. This is a very useful and practical deliverable for everyone in the company as well as for customer ambassadors.

9 **Brand book directions.** The brand book is used mostly for marketing and communication guidance and is usually a digital document, though sometimes it is printed out. It contains a strategy section that includes all the results of brand strategy development processes: the brand mind space, brand positioning, the brand code and motto, the brand activity generator and the brand story.

Deliverable: Brandflight delivers directions on how to develop the brand book. It is usually designed by a designer who already works with the brand, either on products, packaging or user experience (UX). This helps to maintain a uniform design style with other key design elements of the brand.

10 **Customer touch-point coding.** We have invented a practical methodology in order to synchronize the different types of customer touch-point with the brand code and motto, and with the criteria for each touch-point in the four dimensions.

Deliverable: The perfect tool to develop and manage customer touch-points.

11 **The brand launch plan.** The final step in the process is to create an activity plan for how to launch the brand. Separate specialists execute their relevant activities, such as PR specialists, advertising specialists, event specialists and social media specialists who handle media planning, content production and coordination.

Deliverable: A complete and detailed launch plan that covers the actions required by all sections of the company as well as those required by external experts.

▶

Figure 8.2 Brand activity generator: manifesting the brand strategy

Functional activities
New products and services, presentations, sales tools, naming, packaging, design, etc.

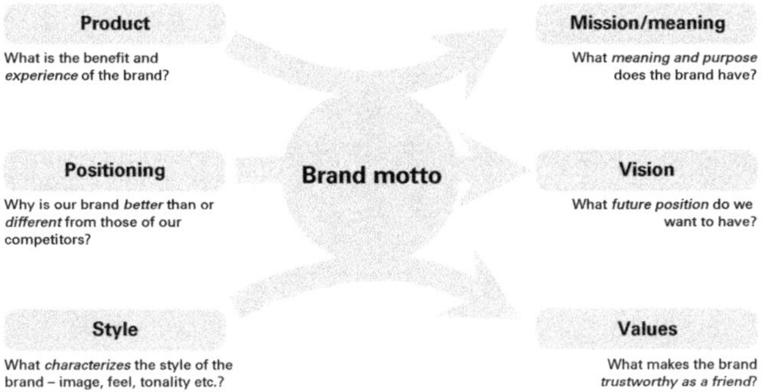

Mental activities
Concepts, mentoring, role modelling, training, etc.

Mission/meaning
What *meaning and purpose* does the brand have?

Vision
What *future position* do we want to have?

Values
What makes the brand *trustworthy as a friend?*

Brand motto

Product
What is the benefit and *experience* of the brand?

Positioning
Why is our brand *better* than or *different* from those of our competitors?

Style
What *characterizes* the style of the brand – image, feel, tonality etc.?

Spiritual (meaning) activities
Communicating the *meaning*: PR, events, sponsoring, involvement, etc.

Social activities
Community, events, sponsoring, etc.

Figure 8.3 The start-up branding process

1 Checking in	2 Fuelling	3 Navigating	4 Taking off	5 Journey
Get briefed up	Get a brand vision	Target your brand	Power your brand code	Activate your brand
Lecture on modern branding	**Brand vision** workshop	**Brand mind space** workshop: • visual • verbal	**Brand code** workshop: • create • control your one-page brand strategy	**Brand activity generator workshop** • testing your brand strategy • creating activities to launch it
Learn about relation branding and how it has changed all we knew previously about branding	Do it like all top performing athletes would do it – see the result before you make it	Create your *expected* brand in people's minds		
				Brand story scripting • create your one-minute brand story
	Do it yourself	Do it yourself	Do it yourself	Share your brand
	Do it yourself			

Conclusion: The brand code is the heart of a brand

Defining the brand code is like tuning an instrument. Sometimes the brand code is nicknamed the DNA code of the brand and this is a very good metaphor. In the same way that DNA can be traced in, and affects the appearance of, all parts of the body, the brand code should be traceable and influential in every part of your business. The brand code is just one vital part of the entire process of creating or coding a brand, as described above. From the brand code and the brand motto that encapsulates and summarizes it, you can begin creating customer experiences that reveal your brand code with every contact your customers have with your company.

Customer experience branding

09

Creating a perceived difference, even if there is none

Customer experience, nowadays often called CX, is very well defined as:

> an interaction between an organization and a customer as perceived through the customer's conscious and subconscious mind. It is a blend of an organization's rational performance and the senses stimulated and emotions evoked, intuitively measured against customer expectations across all moments of contact.
>
> (Shaw and Ivens, 2004)

In a famous quote, Steve Jobs gives his often-repeated view on the order of building a business and on the role that customer experience plays in this: 'You've got to start with the customer experience and work back toward the technology – not the other way around' (Jobs, 1997).

Brand is key to customer experience

The brand strategy (including the value proposition that is part of the brand code) is key to the customer experience.

The customer experience formula is simple, but no less important: Value = Benefits – Cost (including risks and pain). Branding is the management of perception in people's minds, and the sense of value is always a perception.

Your brand code details what you deliver, tangibly and emotionally. It is the basis for your relationship with your customer. All businesses face the risk of losing their sense of what their brand and value proposition really are. This is especially true in situations when the market is changing. New vendors appear, new products suddenly emerge and infringe on your market legacy.

So far, we have focused on the brand and the brand strategy. A good brand strategy should always contain the overreaching idea of how to deliver an extraordinary customer experience. Now, let's leave the strategy for a while and see what it takes to actually produce a different and successful customer experience.

Customer experience is of the utmost importance in today's world where the actual product or service differences have become minimal. It is this focus on the perceived difference that explains how some brands become more successful than others in acquiring the right customers, creating growth and driving word-of-mouth referrals.

The first step to understanding customer experience is to mentally bring customers closer to your business and to understand where and how customer experience influences your success. Companies that understand and systematically review the customer journey and experience of each type of customer enjoy higher customer loyalty and more profitable relationships.

Customer expectations drive customer experience

Branding is all about building the customer experience, and here we encounter one of the most interesting mechanisms in building a high-performing customer experience brand. The relationship between customer expectations and their experiences can be viewed as an equation: Expectation × Delivery = Experience. This means that higher expectations result in a higher overall customer experience and a stronger brand, and lower expectations result in a lower level of customer experience. Even with the same level of positive delivery experience in both cases.

The first case in which I personally observed this customer experience branding mechanism in action comes from the 1980s when Televerket, the Swedish formerly state-owned telecom monopoly, was facing privatization and the change from its status as a state-owned monopoly to becoming a publicly listed and privately owned telecommunications company called Telia. This same privatization and deregulation was occurring in many countries at this time, and the previously state-owned companies had to learn to stand on their own and compete with private alternatives as commercial businesses (Edwardsson, n.d.).

The biggest hurdle Televerket had to face was the universally perceived lack of modern customer service. They had to deal with the issue of suddenly becoming customer service focused. We created an advertising campaign that promised a 'new' Televerket and we supported the big ambition to change the state-owned monopoly into a customer service experience company with very simple activities that were already being taken for granted in the private sector. One of the proofs of change in delivery was that the 'new' Televerket actually called customers after an installation or repair service and asked if the customer was satisfied. Previously, this was unheard of. The people who worked at Televerket while it was still state-owned had behaved much like the civil servants they in effect were – unwilling to ask customers for feedback in the expectation that it would all be negative and cause more trouble.

Our successful work with Televerket taught me a great deal that I have been able to use many times, and not just with other state-owned monopolies facing privatization and deregulation, such as the Swedish state railway company SJ and the nationally owned Scandinavian airline SAS. Of the many things I learned, an important one is that if you communicate an ambition to change, that change begins to take effect in people's minds even before you carry out your plan to change. The communication of the ambition is itself a change-maker.

This is truly branding: managing perceptions in people's minds. I also realized that when the expectation of change or the perceived likelihood that change will occur is low, the more surprising any change is and the more effective it will become. On many occasions, the willingness and desire of a company or brand to change is enough to win goodwill and encouragement from customers and potential customers. We want to think positively and believe in high ambitions, rather than no ambition at all. And we do want to help an ambitious and change-willing business to become a winner. This is especially true if the business delivers something that has become important and needed in our lives and work. We do support the ambitious and expected positive experience, even if delivery is, if we look at it dispassionately, not great.

Why don't more businesses use these mechanisms?

The big blockage that keeps a company from raising expectations on customer experience is that you create a pressure on yourself to live up to and commit to a greater customer experience. This comes partly from a lack of confidence within the organization, and also partly from a lack of risk-taking and commitment. Every company with an aim to become really successful has to deal with this lack of confidence. And the method to doing this begins with raising your own commitment levels, encouraging self-confidence among your employees and allowing them to take more risks.

While financial incentives come quickly to mind for encouraging employees, research shows that the greatest driver towards personal excellence and performance of complex tasks is not monetary incentives (the carrot). Nor is it fear of punishment (the stick), or a combination of the two. The motivational force of purpose or self-satisfaction is a much stronger driving force than either of the obvious choices (Pink, 2010).

Building a confidence culture in an organization starts with building up the individual key people. This can be done using the amazing tool of personal branding, a process of self-evaluation and self-targeting, in combination with coaching. In Chapter 15 you can read more about the surprising powers of individuals, and how they are an essential part of creating positive customer experience branding.

The customer journey

The customer experience branding that we cover in this chapter begins with knowing your customer better. Many companies fail to successfully manage their customer experience branding because they do not emphasize the customer experience in all levels of management. Knowing your customer better is the core idea of customer experience branding, and it begins with understanding, and experiencing, your own brands in the same way that your customers do.

One way to understand your customers' experiences is to systematically study and manage the customer journey. There are many ways to describe the customer journey; the one I use is the customer brand experience lifecycle (Figure 9.1).

This lifecycle begins when customers find you, then learn more about you. They then make their choice and use the product or service they have chosen. After this, customers and users will make an evaluation. As a brand owner, you need to involve your customers, learn how they perceive you and encourage recommendations.

At each stage, there are questions you need to answer in order to provide the best customer experience.

Figure 9.1 The customer brand experience lifecycle

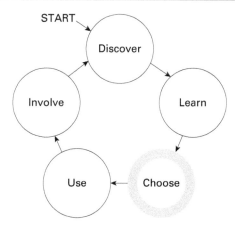

- *Discover:* Where are your customers looking for you?
- *Learn:* What is your customer trying to learn?
- *Choose:* What are the barriers to purchase/usage?
- *Use:* What satisfies/dissatisfies?
- *Involve:* What is your customers' evaluation? Believe only tangible actions like purchases and active recommendations; beware of satisfaction metrics because of their biased, subjective and expressive nature – things people say that seldom lead to actions.

The cornerstones of customer experience

There are four factors that create a sustainable, extraordinary, successful customer experience in any kind of businesses. These four factors, or corner-stones, of customer experience are:

- surprise;
- joy;
- trust;
- respect.

The first of these four success factors – *surprise* – is the main theme of this book. We have already covered surprise in terms of how to handle it. But this book wouldn't be complete, or at least efficient in practice, if we didn't include the other factors of creating an extraordinary customer experience. All of them are important, and enough can be said about each of them to warrant their own books.

We don't have that much space here, so, of necessity, what follows is just the briefest summary of the most important aspects of each factor. The difference between surprise and the others is that surprise, by its nature, is the most unexpected and the least obvious. *Joy*, *trust* and *respect* are classically and commonly accepted as success factors in business. But all four together form the fundament for successful business.

Surprise – the unexpected

As a *surprise* business case, I chose KLM and their experiment of surprising passengers by giving them small, individualized gifts based on each passenger's Twitter or Facebook posts. The smiles of surprise were genuine, because the surprises were both relevant and unexpected. The viral effect of these surprises was huge, with over a million very positive Tweets from one day's activity. You can read more about this experiment in Chapter 12.

Joy – a constant positive reminder

While surprise creates the initial (and periodically updated) 'wow' effect, *joy* is what creates continuity in the pleasant and positive relationship with the brand. When Uber was introduced, it was an amazing surprise to see, live on the screen of your smartphone, your vehicle actually approaching – a joy that never seemed to fade even for loyal, many-times users of Uber.

This repeated joy as a customer and user can be created in many different ways, including using intuitiveness, ease, lightness, smartness, elegance and intelligence among others. Another effective method is the popular concept of 'gamification', a game-like playfulness or amusement that borders on humour.

Another good example is BMW, who focus their brand on joy. For a long time now their brand motto has been 'Joy of Driving', and in their advertising in 2010 BMW made the following statement:

BMW creates joy.
We do not make cars.
We are the creators of emotion.
We are the keepers of thrill.
We are the guardians of one three-letter word: Joy.

(2020BMV, 2015)

When I attended an engineering session at BMW I didn't understand much of their deep technical discussion, full of jargon, but all of a sudden one of the BMW tech people exclaimed in German: 'Aber das hat mit Freude am Fahren gar nichts zu tun!' ('This has nothing to do with the joy of driving!')

It was amazing to experience how the brand idea was maintained in a technical discussion among engineers, yet this was very typical of BMW's brand-guided engineering culture.

Trust – belief in delivery

There are three building blocks on which you create the foundations of *trust*: expectations, needs and promises. I learned this from the real expert on trust, Vanessa Hall who wrote *The Truth About Trust in Business* and holds seminars all over the world to teach us trust (Hall, 2009).

Trust takes place only if all three building blocks are solid and in place, when the:

- *expectations* of your brand are met, or managed;
- *needs* are met;
- *promises* made are kept.

Recognise that every piece of communication, every single ad, every PR event and every branding activity builds up expectations, taps into needs and makes promises that you must fulfil if you want true, sustained success. There is no room for excuses.

It is important to consider all expectations and promises, including the implicit ones as well as the explicit ones. Also, remember that some expectations do not depend on you as brand owner. Some factors are outside your control, but as brand owner you still need to take care of them.

It's important to consider that people are different and have different priorities when it comes to needs. Maslow's hierarchy of needs defines the most important human needs: physiological, safety, social, esteem and self-actualization. Match your different types of customers with those different types of needs.

A good example on the theme of trust is Sephora. This cosmetic retail brand was founded in 1970, in Paris, and introduced to the USA in 1998. It has grown quickly ever since and in 2015 it continued its rise with a double-digit organic revenue growth. Sephora has more than 1,600 points-of-sale, including over 360 locations across North America, and a significant market share despite the hard, established competition from department store retailers like Macy's (LVMH, 2016). Sephora's brand idea is to sell only premium brands and products. Its aim is to be experienced as if it were an independent, trusted advisor.

Through this, Sephora has attracted younger customers, offering a superb customer service that focuses on colour, fragrance and skin care. They also have an effective cross-sell of their products, organized alphabetically while department stores are still organized by brands. In the largely not-very-trustworthy cosmetic world, Sephora is an exception and has gained an amazing relative trust.

Respect – demonstrating empathy and humanism

Respect is, in many ways, the most difficult of the four pillars of customer experience. For a business, respect is the ability to really identify with customer needs, and feel what your customers are feeling. This is easy in theory; most suppliers think they can use their personal experience as customers when delivering products or services. The problem is that you can never really do that. The moment you become a supplier instead of a consumer, you irreversibly change your perspective and lose your independence. You become a producing pro, no longer an innocent user-amateur.

Respect is about being sensitive to the weak customer signals. It's usually about going one step further than expected. This is why I like to use Apple, and particularly Siri, a voice control interface across all Apple products and platforms, as an example of respect in the context of customer experience.

Within the customer experience, better design and easy-to-use products are directly connected to respect for customers. The opposite of respect is arrogance and, when compared with Apple, a lot of tech companies were generally perceived as very arrogant in terms of respecting customers' needs for good design and ease of use. Siri, shows respect for both the needs of users and for the natural human behaviour of users. A voice-interface like Siri is, in many ways, more sensitive and has to be more respectful to differences in culture, tradition and language, which is a great challenge in being respectful to customers and users.

Customer experience and user experience

One of the most important areas today for customer experience is that of digital applications. These digital screens, their content and their user connections are part of almost every customer experience in today's world simply because of our daily and frequent usage of digital devices – in addition to our smartphones, tablets and computers, the screens are in our cars, our household appliances and the machines we use in almost every type of workplace and retail experience.

In the digital development world this is usually called user experience (UX). Because of its dominance in our customer experience branding world I cannot ignore it in this book. I see it as the third generation of brand 'window': the medium through which a brand expresses itself.

Branding has had three important windows in history so far. The first generation brand window was the *packaged* product. Here, I love the example of the tin of Campbell's soup that became an icon of the consumer product for Andy Warhol. The brand was the product, expressed through the packaging; its brand personality was mainly created through the package.

The second generation brand window was *advertising*. In the early years of advertising, the product and package itself were the centre of attention in most advertisements. Gradually, advertising became an expression of the brand, rather than the product. Advertising was, and still is, about animating the brand, making it more emotional and psychological.

The third generation brand window is now the *app*, or rather the user experience of the app. And if you think about it, the app does it all. It not only gives identity to the product or service, it not only communicates and sells the product or service, it is also part of the product or service. Because it is truly integrated with the customer, the product or service and the brand, it activates what the business of the product or service stands for. The app interactively helps animate the brand in a user dialog. It shifts the brand from a product-centred transaction brand to a modern, interactive relation brand.

During my cooperation with Idean, one of the leading and fastest growing companies in the world of UX, people with hands-on experience, including founder and owner Risto Lahdesmaki, have taught me the importance and requirements of what makes a good app and user experience. Risto is one of the best user experience creators in the world, and with his input I developed a new methodology for creating the ultimate brand user experience (BUX).

Brand user experience

This method is built on relation branding and uses 4-D branding to create brands and apps that fit perfectly together and meet the needs of today's users. As this third generation of brand windows is obviously interactive it allows a new level of interaction and a relationship between the customer and the brand through its digital user interface. Therefore, managing the digital brand user experience becomes as important as managing the rest of the customer experience.

In addition to applying the general rules of creating a good customer experience, there are three steps you need to consider to make an app work well:

1 **Customer/user ethnography.** Find out what the customer and user wants and needs, not only when using the app, but also in a larger context, what the customer wants out of life.

   In order to do this, you need a few deep investigative interviews with your customers and users at their homes or workplaces. You need to be able to monitor the weak signals and you need to find out what the emotional-psychological resonance of your app is and use that knowledge to create an app that is surprisingly better, more liked and more used than any of your competitors'.

2 **Relation brand strategy for your app.** In order to make your app work better and become more popular, you need to build it on a modern brand strategy that does your brand justice. Here, you have to switch from old transaction brand, product-focused thinking to the new school of relation branding. I have used my powerful 4-D branding successfully on hundreds of businesses. Your brand cannot just have a functional dimension any more, but must also have the social dimension, mental dimension and spiritual dimension. Your app will then be equipped with what it takes to become the most loved and used app... and your brand will too!

3 **Brand user experience.** When designing and coding the UX of an app, you need to include all of the above. The weak signals from your anthropological interviews reveal users' intimate thoughts and lead you to small, but important, details. The app must create relationships in your users' minds, making them feel at home, charming them, pampering and respecting them. The app must be attractive to your customers, in the same way that good furniture or a car design can make people love their objects. But it must also stimulate users to do more (and buy more) and feel good about it.

All this can only be done with a lot of experience in the design team, not only of the technological opportunities available in different operative systems, but also with an essential humanistic, aesthetic and cultural approach brought in from the customer/user anthropology (step 1) and the brand strategy (step 2).

Measuring success in customer experience branding

In my opinion, the best and simplest way to measure Customer Experience Branding is by using the Net Promoter Score, or NPS (Figure 9.2). Introduced by Rob Markey and Fred Reichheld from Bain & Company in 2003, the NPS is calculated based on responses to one single question: 'How likely is it that you would recommend us to a friend or colleague?' (Markey and Reichheld, 2011).

This is generally scored on a 0 to 10 scale, with 0 being not at all likely to recommend the product and 10 being extremely likely to do so. Those who respond with a score of 9 or 10 are called 'promoters'. These are the customers who are likely to buy more, remain customers for longer and, most importantly, make more positive referrals to potential customers. Respondents who give a score of 0 to 6 are called 'detractors'. They are less likely to display the positive behaviours that add value to your company. Those who respond with scores of 7 or 8 are called 'passives'. As their name implies, they are neither likely nor unlikely to display the desired positive behaviours.

To calculate the NPS you subtract the percentage of detractors from the percentage of promoters. While passives do affect the total number of respondents, they don't directly affect the NPS.

Companies who use the NPS usually follow up with putting open-ended questions before the individual respondents, asking them to explain why they chose the score they did. These answers are important when deciding follow-up action, and are usually relayed to front-line employees and

Figure 9.2 Brand audit – net promoter score

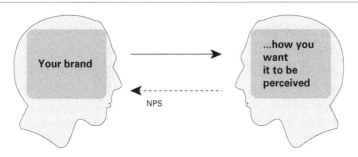

Net promoter score (NPS) is the best way to measure the strength of a brand. In NPS only *one* question is asked, but answers may be followed up individually and analysed.
Q: Would you recommend this brand to a friend?
A: Yes or No

management teams. Additional questions can also be included. These can be used to help understand how the company, product or service is perceived. When using the NPS system, companies often rely on software to help minimise human bias in analysis. Software also often provides a full suite of metrics and reports, as well as the analytics section.

The NPS is mainly used to evaluate customer loyalty to a brand or company. This enables the company to determine the likelihood that customers will buy again, speak positively about the company or resist pressure to switch to a competitor company or brand. However, to be fully effective, the NPS system also needs a process to 'close the loop' and to learn more from customers who have provided feedback. This gives you a chance to turn a negative perception around, to turn a detractor into a promoter.

Internally, the net promoter approach can be used to motivate your organization to focus more on improving your products and services with customer needs in mind. Critics of the NPS mainly dispute its claim that a company's NPS correlates with its revenue growth. It often does, but possibly not with the highest precision. Despite this, and other criticisms, many major companies openly admit that they use the NPS approach, including Siemens, Philips, Apple Stores, GE, American Express and Intuit.

In addition to using the NPS to measure brand loyalty or loyalty to your company, service or physical product, it can also measure loyalty to online apps and social gaming products.

Conclusion: Customer experience branding is all about creating and delivering on expectations

In our super-interconnected world, customer experience is now perceived as more important than ever. It fuels acquisition, drives word-of-mouth referrals and ensures that the right customers are retained (or the wrong ones are pushed away). The first step towards bringing customers closer to your business is to understand where and how customer experience influences your success. Companies that understand and systematically review the journey and experience of each type of customer enjoy higher loyalty and better and more profitable customer relationships. Customer experience can best be created as surprise, based on expectations, and the loyalty generated can be measured using the NPS and the question: Would you recommend this brand to your friend?

References

2020BMV (2015) An inside look at the branding success of BMW [Blog] 2020 Brand + Marketing Visionaries, 30/9. [Online] www.2020bmv.com/ [Last accessed 6.2.16]

Edwardsson, A (n.d.) Liberalization of the telephony markets. [Online] www.teliasonerahistory.com/ [Last accessed: 6.2.16]

Hall, V (2009) *The Truth About Trust in Business: How to enrich the bottom line, improve retention, and build valuable relationships for success*, Emerald Book Company, Austin

Jobs, S (1997) 16 brilliant insights from Steve Jobs [Video and transcript], Keynote Circa 1997. [Online] onstartups.com/ [Last accessed: 23.2.16]

LVMH (2016) 2015 full year results and 2015 financial documents. [Online] www.lvmh.com/investors/publications/ [Last accessed: 23.2.16]

Markey, R and Reichheld, F (2011) Introducing: the Net Promoter System, Bain and Company. [Online] www.bain.com/ [Last accessed: 6.2.16]

Pink, DH (2010) *Drive: The surprising truth about what motivates us*, Riverhead Books, New York

Shaw, C and Ivens, J (2004) Building great customer relationship, in *Building Great Customer Experiences (Beyond Philosophy)*, Palgrave MacMillan, pp 35–36

Customer experience touch-points

10

The points of customer contact

The next step is to explore customer touch-points: all the physical and communication interactions your customers experience during their relationship with your company. Today's market has seen an explosion in the number of customer touch-points, driven by a new awareness of the omni-channel nature of today's marketing. This has greatly increased the complexity of customer relationships, which makes acquiring and retaining customers more difficult than ever. Each increase in touch-point complexity also increases the time, expense and skills required to manage the touch-points.

Customer touch-points are your brand's points of customer contact, from start to finish. Every time customers find your business online or in an advertisement, see ratings and reviews, visit your website, shop at your retail store or contact your customer service they connect with your customer touch-points. This may seem like a long list, but these are just a few of all the possible touch-points. Touch-points occur every time customers come into contact with or 'touch' your brand and anything associated with it.

Individually, sequentially, and in groups, these touch-points define the landscape between the customer's world and the world of the brand owner. The product or service is obviously a touch-point that can communicate much more than just its functionality. However, the most successful companies are moving the customer experience beyond the simple physical user attributes to a more emotional and bonding, and more human, experience.

The static, human, and digital touch-points that make up your brand are defined by your brand strategy and they drive your customer experience. *Static touch-points* are one-way, traditional touch-points, such as the product or service itself, promotion, direct communication, advertising and public relations. *Human touch-points* are two-way, or bilateral, and typically include call centres, service and support, claims, sales and management contacts. *Digital touch-points* are multi-lateral contacts between customers, sometimes excluding the brand owner entirely. These include websites that enable interaction, blogs, user groups, emails, social media and mobile in-app communication. All these brand-driven touch-points contribute to the total customer experience.

It is impressive how some brands have differentiated their products or concepts with a personal touch, and offer an unexpected touch-point experience. One small example of how to humanize touch-points is the guest book in Virgin Atlantic's First Class. By offering such a guest book, the company treats you as a house-guest and not as a passenger. Here, you can put your name next to the names of famous people and celebrities, adding to your experience.

Go-Pro has also personalized its customer experience by basing its entire marketing on customer participation and inclusion. The customers are part of the product.

Figure 10.1 The customer brand touch-point card: customer experience touch-points

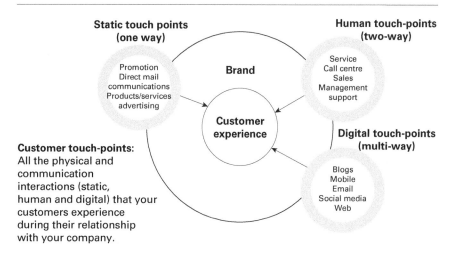

Coding the customer touch-points with your brand code

One of the great ways to activate your brand is to use your brand code to 'code' your customer touch-points. I have developed a simple model for this that I call 'brand touch-point cards'. The first step is to create a one-page card that clearly displays your brand code. Then, using the 4-D brand mind space model, you simply note the touch-point criteria for each customer touch-point.

Customer touch-point card: Google Search – legal documents

For this example we look at how you can fill in these touch-point cards for one of the digital customer touch-points, Google Search (Figure 10.2).

Google Search is one of the most important digital customer touch-points in today's world. It is very often the point at which a potential customer first becomes aware of your brand, by searching for a solution to their current need. To begin analysing this touch-point, let your brand code and motto inspire the search engine optimisation (SEO) management of your landing page. The brand code guides your customer's search experience. It defines the 4-D touch-point criteria for the entire Google Search customer experience, as well as the development of the landing page on your brand's website.

The example is for a successful online legal advice and document business. In this case, the spiritual dimension had no relevant criteria.

- **The functional criteria:** On the landing page, use as much key information as possible while considering the Google Search result (SEO). Example legal keywords: will, purchase contract, inheritance, employment contract, lease contract. Each keyword should be directed to a landing page with direct, and keyword-relevant, information. Each landing page should be linked to a special offer and more information. Build a well-choreographed, rich funnel of target information relevant to the legal keywords.

- **The social criteria:** Landing pages should include special, linked testimonials that pick up on the searched keyword, as well as stories, videos and Facebook links/likes that build on the respective search word.

Figure 10.2 The SmartLaw customer touch-point card: Google Search

Functional criteria

The benefit, product, delivery, offering of the touch-point.

Use the Google Search result as much as possible with key information (search engine optimization), example legal key words: will, buying contract, inheritance, work contracts, lease contract… directed to landing page with direct information about the searched key word… in the landing place linked to special offer and more information. Well choreographed funnel.

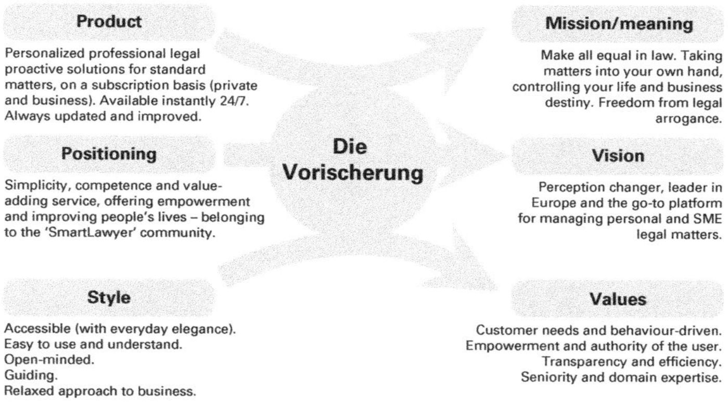

Mental activities

The individual relation effect of the touch-point; personal content, advice, attention, self-confidence and self-awarding elements.

Feeling of getting a personal answer to a personal question, continuation on landing page: explain the 'Vorsicherung' preventing concept features for you as an individual. Introduce relevant questionnaire questions. You can buy a will and three months' membership and receive an updated document.

Product

Personalized professional legal proactive solutions for standard matters, on a subscription basis (private and business). Available instantly 24/7. Always updated and improved.

Mission/meaning

Make all equal in law. Taking matters into your own hand, controlling your life and business destiny. Freedom from legal arrogance.

Positioning

Simplicity, competence and value-adding service, offering empowerment and improving people's lives – belonging to the 'SmartLawyer' community.

Die Vorischerung

Vision

Perception changer, leader in Europe and the go-to platform for managing personal and SME legal matters.

Style

Accessible (with everyday elegance).
Easy to use and understand.
Open-minded.
Guiding.
Relaxed approach to business.

Values

Customer needs and behaviour-driven.
Empowerment and authority of the user.
Transparency and efficiency.
Seniority and domain expertise.

Social activities

The collective identification, group- and community-building elements of the touch-point, reviews, references and opinions.

(On landing page:) special linked testimonials picking up the searched word (the 'SmartLawyers' community), stories, videos, Facebook links/likes.

Spiritual criteria

The purpose and meaning connection of the touch-point:

reminding customers that the brand is engaged in and concerned about creating a better world.

(On landing page:) access for everybody to good law support and advice.

- **The mental/individual criteria:** Landing pages should provide a feeling of getting a personal answer to a personal question, with continuation on the landing page. Explain the concept features relevant to the visitor as an individual. Introduce relevant questionnaire questions and, for instance, a personal offer of three months' membership, updated documents and educational information when you buy a will document.

Apple's customer touch-points

Another example of a very successful champion of customer experience is Apple. Michelle Greenwald, a contributor to *Forbes*, revealed her list of the top customer experience touch-points that Apple does well (Greenwald, 2014) and I find that this is a good example to study, because it covers many different aspects of the branding, from online contact points and packaging to retail and human interaction.

- **A well-designed website:** Apple's website design is simple and elegant. Navigation is intuitive and well laid out, which makes it easy to find information about upcoming and existing products, locate your nearest Apple Store and set up business appointments.

- **Packaging:** Apple has put a lot of effort into packaging and delivering their products. The packaging has been designed with quality and luxury in mind. Such a simple thing as the way the boxes open, and the products are displayed within the boxes, conveys a sense that there is something special about the product. The packaging can also be clever, as with the shopping bags with cords that can be used as a backpack, or with the computer packages with carry handles that act as billboards when customers carry their purchases home.

- **In-store demo units:** In addition to employees in each Apple Store who are there to explain and demonstrate each product, the existence of demo units that customers can try out adds to the pleasurable customer experience. Letting customers test products before they buy is a very effective marketing tactic, and Apple make this easy.

- **Employee density, attitudes and training:** With plenty of employees in each Apple Store, customers are assured of quick assistance. There are no long waits for service or information. Apple also carefully selects and trains candidates to ensure their in-store employees are smart, patient, knowledgeable and solution-oriented.

- **Apple Store design and layout:** Even the consistent design of the Apple Stores shows Apple's commitment to providing an excellent customer experience. Apple Stores are kept clean and clutter-free, with bags, receipt printers and other necessary supplies out of sight beneath display tables. The cheerful lighting and uniform, elegant design contribute to a familiar and positive experience.

- **Location:** All Apple Stores aim to be located in areas frequented by their relatively well-education customers. They are all easy to find and easy to access.

- **The Genius Bar:** The Genius Bar, offered at some Apple Stores, provides instant support and help for your Apple products. Here, you can get help troubleshooting hardware issues and discuss any repair options that may be necessary. In some cases, repairs may even be carried out while you wait. This personal and direct access to support staff makes grateful customers fans for life.

- **One to One tutorials:** With each purchase of a computer, customers are offered an additional One to One service that provides tutorials for a two-year period after the purchase. Customers can schedule trainings sessions of various lengths with Apple specialists, and learn how to effectively use the both the hardware and software.

- **Acknowledging appointments:** Apple sends a confirmation email to customers who have made appointments at Apple Stores. This simple service makes customers feel noticed, reminds them of their appointment and reduces the number of no-shows.

- **Staff collaboration:** Whether you seek assistance at a Genius Bar or through the One to One training sessions, if an Apple employee is unsure of the answer he or she will readily collaborate with other employees to find a solution. This ability to seek assistance assures customers that there is a full team at their disposal that is able to solve any problem.

- **Short waiting times:** Many Apple Stores employees have a mobile cash register in their hands, which reduces check-out times and makes purchases more seamless.

- **Personal Setup:** This service ensures that customers understand how to use their new devices before they leave the Apple Store. Showing customers exactly how to get the most out of what they have just bought not only makes customers happier and more excited about their purchase, it also reduces customer service expenses later on.

- **In-store classes:** If the Personal Setup service is not enough, some Apple Stores also offer regularly schedules classes that explain the basics of device usage and highlight the most useful software features. This increases customer appreciation of the products and brand.

- **In-store events:** With in-store events, including classes and guest speakers, Apple increases traffic to the store while enhancing customer participation and increasing the likelihood that visitors will purchase something else. On an emotional level, customers feel that Apple helps them, entertains them and empowers them.

- **Acknowledging rebate receipts:** When Apple has rebate offers, it sends a confirmation email informing customers that the rebate request has been received and is being processed. This provides peace of mind and ensures that the customer feels that their needs are being taken care of.

- **Software development kits:** In the beginning, Apple created all the hardware and software for all its products. With the release of software development kits (SDKs), over one million apps have been developed by fans and other companies. Not only does this allow software developers to distribute and sell their apps globally, but it also gives customers and fans access to a huge variety of useful and fun apps that make their devices an integral and valued part of their lives.

- **Satisfaction questionnaire:** When a customer makes a new purchase, Apple will often send a request to fill out a satisfaction questionnaire. This allows Apple to continuously improve each aspect of the customer experience. It also gives the customer the feeling that their input and feedback is desired by and useful to Apple.

Conclusion: A customer experience brand is as strong as the sum of its customer touch-points

From Apple's example, we can learn how a brand can win the loyalty and devotion of its customers. When your own people understand the customer experience, and even experience it as customers do, they can contribute to improving the experience and the product, and making it more personal, more pleasant and more productive. To fully understand the touch-points your customers routinely experience, you can create a 'touch-point map' or 'journey map' that details all the contact points before, during and after purchase. When you have this, try to think beyond the obvious – surprise and delight your customer. In many cases, effective touch-point management can reduce customer service costs. It can also reduce advertising costs by encouraging customer interaction and favourable word-of-mouth advertising. The time and money you spend on touch-point management can yield the highest returns of any marketing strategy.

References

Greenwald, M (2014) 20 ways Apple masters customer touchpoints and why it's great for business, *Forbes*, 21 May. [Online] www.forbes.com/ [Last accessed: 6.2.16]

Brand play   11
The implementation and dramaturgy of customer experience branding

Brand communication is no longer just a marketing or exercise. Brands still need to perform; they still need to satisfy all their stakeholders – the customers, employees, journalists, investors – and they still need to keep the conversation going. However, the method now needs to be more individualistic and intelligent. The era of sending out messages only is gone.

One-way communication dominated the world of transaction branding. Single messages were broadcast with the aim of hammering a message into people's heads, to condition them. The focus was on the message and on using the right channel to target the right individuals or groups.

In the modern world audiences are fragmented and becoming immune to this tactic of 'one message fits all', so a different approach is needed. The current strategy works with themes and stories, reaching people directly and involving them. Instead of targeting audiences, today's powerful, full-potential branding needs to respect people as separate, social individuals with their own ideas, interest and priorities. Today's branding needs to reach people who, directly or indirectly, interact as participants in bigger, ongoing conversations with a lot of other people.

Nowadays, communication demands the full attention of the whole organization in a business, including top management. Conversations surround and often bypass the brand. They can irritate and sometimes harm the brand. Quite often, the view that a brand has of itself and the view stakeholders have of the brand are in conflict.

In order to deal with these conflicts, a deeper involvement is needed. Brands need to partner with the world. They need to go out and listen, bring the world and their customers into the corporation and create a portfolio of inspiring opportunities to involve people. The brand needs to be in touch with the people's daily life and develop platforms for conversation. People have become more independent and flexible. Expectations and interests grow, conflicts and experiences are visible to everyone through the everyday use of social media, as well as the connections between online and traditional media. Hidden secrets become the exceptions. The world is more various and more complex, and brands need to consider this in their strategies.

Content and dramaturgy

The implementation of a brand strategy consists of two parts. One is the conversation content and the other is the dramaturgy or the dramatic composition of the implementation. Obviously, surprise is crucial when you set up a brand and launch it. Yet, in order to keep the branding and the business going, there is also a need for a continued implementation dramaturgy that includes scripted surprise. The customer experience themes have to be prepared and worked with to become effective. In my practice, I felt the need to develop tools to manage today's brand implementation, with all new demands taken into consideration. The two most powerful tools that I use are the brand conversation map and the brand experience script. Let's take a closer look at those.

The brand conversation map

The brand conversation map is a new methodology that connects the brand platform (brand mind space, brand code and brand activity generator) with resonating conversations that support effective branding and allow it to reach its full potential. It's focused on the content of storytelling and on interaction between people, privately or in their business, linked by the brand.

Social media is a two-way approach that can be used to both listen to people and give them a platform to engage themselves. In order to support these brand conversations, which occur mostly in social media, we can use the brand conversation map. This tool also helps initiate and manage those conversations in a more systematic way.

Regardless of any communication channel, the brand communication map follows a 'content first' premise. Themes and stories allow the brand to address all four dimensions of the brand mind space and form a grand brand narrative. They link the conversations, cluster and focus the brand activities and define a narrative strategy. The brand can effectively and efficiently be anchored in people's minds. Consistent communication patterns will form, will become unique to the brand and will drive brand recognition and loyalty. The themes in the brand conversation map are not meant for direct one-way communication; they are true multi-channel communication themes designed to inspire, inform, facilitate and co-ordinate marketing and communication tactics in a new and different, individual way.

The brand conversation map is the main marketing tool for relation brands, and it is based on the following four core premises, disrupting the traditional transaction branding approach.

1 **From marketing communication to brand conversation.** Relation brands care a great deal about engaging in conversations. This means not only maintaining a direct dialogue with partners, customers, media and the public, but also listening and anticipating, and then engaging with meaningful activities. The power has shifted from a sales-driven monologue to relationship-building conversations with several parties at the same time. This also means that the brand conversation is not owned by the marketing function alone. Instead, all touch-points with people (external and internal) need to be involved and contribute to bring emotion to the brand and make it come alive. This also has another effect: it's not about a single core message (however well orchestrated). Instead, it's about forming consistent message patterns.

2 **From campaigns to themes and stories marketing.** The transactional branding model tried to capture the essence of the brand using visual and verbal communication (logo, slogan, picture) and big campaigns. But the true value of brands lies in the meaning it has for the people who interact with it. Brand communication has become a multifaceted dialogue: people talk with people – and occasionally with brands. So a meaningful approach is needed, in order to enter into a conversation between people, and to be a partner rather than a disturber. Brands need to resonate with deeper value patterns. And here, the currency is trust. Themes should connect with the value patterns and with the brand code, and build the foundation of the brand conversation map. What you gain from this is a new, inclusive form of brand storytelling.

3 **From being simplistic to informed simplicity.** Two approaches fail to engage in conversations in a meaningful manner and enable full-potential branding: ignoring today's complexity; and producing an incoherent accumulation of activities that do not follow a deeper logic. With the brand conversation map, a brand can facilitate participation and promotion through providing content and experiences that involve people in co-authoring an overall grand brand narrative. Brand themes tie together activities and allow the brand to express various facets. The brand conversation map structure ensures consistency through 'informed simplicity'

– a term used among architects and software engineers to simplify something complex by creating clarifying patterns within the complex structures (Frederick, 2007).

4 **Towards involvement and co-authoring.** Transmedia storytelling has many names: transmedia narrative, multi-platform storytelling or cross-media seriality. Whatever you choose to called it, this is the technique of telling a single story or story experience across multiple platforms and formats using current digital technologies. It enables deeper involvement with certain aspects of the brand. It is a shift from monologue (one-to-one) past dialogue (one-to-many) to conversations between several (many-to-many and one in-between). The brand has to live with no longer being in control of all ongoing conversations, and needs to find ways to balance with letting things go with the flow. The task is to create multiple entry points for people to get in contact with the brand. The brand's role is to provide platforms for individual and collective brand experiences, as well as outlets for co-creation that encourage sharing and engaging. The brand conversation map is a concept that allows exactly this.

Transmedia storytelling and how it works

Just as in the process of creating the brand code, where diverse inputs contribute to a robust brand platform, transmedia storytelling contributes to a conversation platform that carries the power of the *brand code*.

Transmedia storytelling in brand conversation focuses on stories and on the characters playing the stories. Just as the brand code is carefully developed to guarantee a consistent understanding of the brand, transmedia storytelling is created to guarantee a consistent communication of the brand in a more involving and interesting way. The story is created like a network with different stories across different media.

Brand themes: The connection between the brand platform and the mega trends

For many brands, mega-trends are a central strategic issues that, for example, sets a business area focus. So Nike's 'The Consumer Decides' is one of 11 maxims in the corporate strategy and it is connected to a mega-trend through which individualization reaches a new level (Greene, 2008). It is also a clear demonstration of how the power balance has shifted: consumers create their own portfolio of interests and networks. In the brand conversation map, we call these connections brand themes. They literally draw a line between the positioning today and the vision for tomorrow.

The mega-trends themselves are broad and they need to be meaningful for the brand. At the same time, the brand also needs to create meanings to have a place in people's lives. A brand theme represents part of the meaning, the central idea of the brand, and is not directly stated most of the time, but is implicit in all brand activities and expressions. The themes support the balance between being in touch with people while maintaining control over the brand.

The brand experience script: The dramaturgy of brand activation

Surprise should appear to be spontaneous and unexpected. But what is often forgotten is that there also needs to be a continual drama to keep the relation brand, and the business, going. Successful surprise has to be sequentially repetitive and thus planned and scripted. The doom that falls when a once-surprising brand seems to be running out of its surprise-steam is hard. Surprise is the fuel for today's relation brands.

Marketers typically spend the bulk of their creative energy making themselves look attractive to potential customers. It's easy to forget you need to look sexy and charming to your current customers as well to keep the spark alive. As chief marketing officers (CMOs) push their staffs and agencies to be faster, cheaper and more accountable, they also need to push the brand organization to be more surprising.

When we study brands like Nokia and Apple, we can see what happens when the surprises stop coming. The first lost its position because it lost its ability to continually surprise. Apple suffered a news silence of nearly two years and was in serious danger of losing its magic (Gustin, 2013). Fortunately, Tim Cook ensured Apple's recovery by releasing a battery of 'surprising' yet pre-announced products (O'Brien, 2013).

Apple shows that a brand has an amazing ability to recover its perception of being surprising and inventive in our minds. However, when nothing unexpected has happened for a longer time, disappointment turns into malice, and the downturn has to be completely disrupted. A new flow of surprises is urgently needed to recover the brand, and they often need to occur in a different build-up of the four dimensions than the brand has used before.

How long this period of non-surprise can be before a brand loses its ability to recover is never clear. It is a complex issue, and individual for each brand. Generally, a brand is able to recover after a year or two of non-surprise, but few modern brands will survive longer than three years of no new surprises.

The brand experience script is the structure of continued brand activation

The inspiration for what I call the 'brand experience script takes the structure of a screenplay. In this I have been inspired by Syd Field, author of *The Screenwriter's Workbook* and an authority in Hollywood and beyond. The structure he outlines in his book is present in almost every movie produced all over the world (Field, 1984).

The dramatic development of the brand is what enables it to enter our minds, or our hearts. As Swedish director Ingmar Bergman used to say, 'the language of the cinema speaks directly to the heart' (Field, 1984).

It is in building and executing the story of a brand that we create its positions in our minds and enable a strong, successful relation brand to become a preferred, loved and trusted friend. The relation brand needs a different methodology from the transaction brand, which was purely focusing on the functional dimension of the direct product benefits. Transaction brand communication was built on pushing product arguments and slightly modified key product features. They constantly repeated the same kind of messages until they were stored in our brains.

Creating relationships with a relation brand implies that the customers have to open up an emotional space for the brand, to let it become a friend, and that the brand has to win customer sympathy step by step. This works in exactly the same way that good lead characters in a movie or TV series win our sympathy through their personality, will and ambition. This drive in the script, as filmmakers call it, provides a goal, purpose or meaning we can sympathise with.

When you write a screenplay you need to know your main characters well (product, style, values). You also need to know the plot, including how the story begins (positioning) and how it ends (vision). All this script material is supplied by your brand code, making it easier to script your brand experience script. Below, you can see how the brand code delivers all these ideas and information. The brand code is to the brand story what the central story idea of a movie is to the film script. Where does the story start, where and how does it end and what is its purpose and meaning?

- The *product* is the introduction of the main character (the brand).
- The *positioning* is where the main character stands now. In what way is the lead character different from others (including ambition)?
- The *vision* is the goal and the end of the story. Where will the main character be, and what will the character be like, in 10 to 15 years?
- The *style* is the personal traits and personality of the main character.
- The *values* are the main character's beliefs and most important guiding rules in life.
- The *mission/meaning* is the main character's purpose in life. What does the main character want to achieve?

Scripting the brand experience script

The brand experience script follows the classic three-act structure used by many plays and films. In act I the current situation is revealed and the story develops towards the first turning point, the first plot-point. The action and conflicts are developed in act II, and resolved in act III, the final act.

Act I: Set-up

Here, the brand introduces itself, including how it is different (positioning), and what its ambitions are. It reveals its personality (style and values), and we begin to understand what drives the brand, what its goal might be (vision) and what its purpose might be (mission/meaning). At the end of act I we have plot-point 1, in which the development of the brand turns in a surprising direction. This could be anything from entering a new market geography to devising a new application of the product, or a new usage in a new context. With relation brands, the surprise can be as simple as a new and interesting method of interacting with its audience through social media, or a new way of communicating or acting out the brand's purpose and meaning. Such activities manifest all the four dimensions of the brand.

Act II: Confrontation

The second act covers the main action and 'conflicts' of the brand; how the brand overcomes hurdles on its way to reach its goal (vision). A brand typically has to deal with competitors, with challenging people's traditional views or perceptions, with showing what it can do to change things that the competitors maybe can't or haven't yet done. It's a saga about how the brand becomes preferred, loved and used by many satisfied and happy customers. At the end of act II we have plot-point 2. Again, the brand takes a new and surprising turn. This time, it can be any surprising change in the life of the brand, like entering into a new category, co-branding with another brand, introducing a new brand product or offering a different usage to new customers and users.

Act III: Resolution

Here, the brand ties up the loose ends from act II and ends this part in the series, while providing an opportunity for a continuation. Plot-point 2 prepares for the resolution in every movie and every episode of a TV series. And the resolution offers an opportunity to continue in many more episodes to come.

A brand experience script in many episodes

That is what you need to keep in mind when creating your brand experience script; it is much more like creating a TV series than creating a movie. You need to create a brand experience script for each episode in a series of episodes. While each episode follows the structure of a movie, the episodes are also tied together in a longer 'plot arc': an overarching story that covers many episodes, over several years. As such, any brand experience script creator will benefit from having a script that outlines how to play the brand over each period, which typically lasts two to three years. But remember, it is very important that you leave the structure open to new, unexpected ideas and changes.

In a brand experience script, each episode is usually a full year. So, each year will contain act I (the set-up and plot-point 1), act II (the confrontation and plot-point 2) and act III (the resolution and provision for continuation).

The following year, and episode, will then begin with a set-up that references previous episodes even as it introduces the current starting position, goals and ambitions. And the cycle continues with this episode, and all episodes that follow.

This structure is clearly visible when Apple's Chief Executive Officer, Tim Cook, starts a twice-a-year show (Apple, 2015). First, he returns to the previous challenges and proudly reports extraordinary results, before he takes on the next episodes with new products and services, or improved existing ones. Apple brilliantly mixes various types of surprises – new products, new relationships with partners or a special music or film offering for all its customers. The innovativeness of surprise is the name of the game.

Systematic delivery of surprises

It is important in the relation brand world to systematically deliver surprises over and over again. So, creating a programme for inventing new ones (using all of the four dimensions, of course!) and planning a routine on how to introduce them becomes paramount. Remember when you were a child anticipating a birthday surprise. As true, loyal fans and friends of a brand, we expect, unfortunately for today's businesses, our brands to perform this same surprise routine, over and again, just as our parents once did. Or they didn't, and let us down.

A simpler, less ambitious version of the brand experience script

If you find the above a little too ambitious and complex for your brand and business, you can simplify it to at least one surprise launch every year. When you do this, you can move around in the brand mind space and produce a functional surprise the first year, a mental surprise the second year, a social surprise the third year and a spiritual surprise the fourth year. In the fifth year, you return to a functional surprise.

If your business requires more frequent functional surprises, you may have to work with that, but you can combine each functional surprise with any of the other dimensions. In this way, you create variety, a broader base for the impact of your marketing and a stronger and deeper relation brand building effect.

Enter the chief surprise officer

Unfortunately, there isn't much in the way of academic research or enterprise-grade software to help companies make surprises happen. Which means it really becomes a question of individual imagination and bravery as well as making sure you are open to situations where you might be surprised yourself.

Birchbox, a subscription service that sends customers a box of mystery beauty products each month, and Phish, the rock band that never performs the same show twice, show that entire business models can be built around the concept of surprise.

But who is responsible for the surprises of a brand? Of course, it has to be the chief executive officer (CEO). At the end of the day, the CEO is responsible for everything in the company. This has to include the continuation of surprise, especially since this a crucial success factor for the brand.

But the CEO can't do everything, all the time. Since surprise is so important for the brand, it's reasonable to have someone who can focus on that responsibility – and the title of chief surprise officer (CSO) comes readily to mind. This could also be an additional responsibility for a chief marketing officer or for a chief brand manager. I encourage you to find a person on a higher level in the company to be the CSO.

In many companies, there is also a chief quality officer or chief sustainability officer. With the dramatic shift from the old-school transaction brands to today's relation brands, quality and sustainability have become matters that any company is expected to do well. The risks of failing on quality and sustainability today, with social media watching you constantly, are immense. With thousands or hundreds of thousands of eyes and ears, and the ability to report instantly to the rest of the world, any case of bad quality or poor sustainability is quickly known and widely reported.

Conclusion: The customer experience brand has to be programmed with systematic surprises

Today's brand conversations in new media channels and on live events require planning tools different from those used for yesterday's mechanical push marketing. Content and dramaturgy have to be produced for new media channels. This chapter takes a look at how. We are introduced to two perfect tools creating content and dramaturgy. The brand conversation map, inspired by the underground transit maps in big cities, lays out themes, characters, plots and storylines. And the brand experience script, inspired by scriptwriting for movies and TV series, pulls it all together in a unified, ongoing brand story.

References

Apple (2015) Apple – September event 2015. [Video, online] www.youtube.com/ [Last accessed: 27.2.16]

Field, S (1984) *The Screenwriter's Workbook*, Dell Publishing Company, New York

Frederick, M (2007) *101 Things I Learned in Architecture School*, The MIT Press, Cambridge, MA

Greene, J (2008) Marketing Innovation Nike Plus presentation, SlideShare, slide 3 of 25. [Online] http://www.slideshare.net/johneire/marketing-innovation-nike-plus-presentation [Last accessed: 12.1.16]

Gustin, S (2013) How far can the mighty Apple fall?, *Time*, 18 April. [Online] business.time.com/ [Last accessed: 27.2.16]

O'Brien, C (2013) What the iPhone 5s and 5c launch taught us about Tim Cook and Apple, *Los Angeles Times*, 22 September. [Online] articles.latimes.com/ [Last accessed: 27.2.16]

Social media branding   12

The single most important differentiator between old school branding and today's Relation brands

Research has shown that, despite many of us are having hundreds of online friends, we spend 80 per cent of our time communicating online with the same 8–10 friends (Dunbar, 2013). Research on social networks also shows that these networks are first used to strengthen existing relationships, rather than to build new relationships. In fact, the more people see each other in person and communicate by phone, the more they communicate online. What we get from these few friends that we communicate with regularly is a very strong support for (or against) our decisions. Often this is done through the subconscious study of our friends and learning and gaining inspiration from their behaviour patterns. In many cases, we may not even realize how much our friends influence us: if your friends are happy, you are more likely to be happy.

This influence is also demonstrated by car-buying habits. People often buy cars based on what others around them are driving. Social proof can be used to guide us towards the preferred course of an action or appropriate behaviour. And this influence affects us far more when we perceive the people around us to be like ourselves. The effect increases disproportionately when people compare themselves with others who are like them, whether they are of a similar age, ethnicity, background or ability (Fogg, 2003).

People are most influenced by the people they are emotionally closest to. These are the people they communicate with the most, socialize with the most, and trust the most. Marketing generally, and in social media specifically, needs to focus on strong ties and the many small, independent, connected groups of friends. It's very hard to find people with a large degree of influence over many others – if they exist at all (Boase *et al*, 2006).

All of us are very influential on some topics, and all of us have a little influence on other topics. All of us can spread messages, because we all connect multiple independent groups of friends together. Instead of trying to find a few people that we think are influential to many, it is better to find many people we don't know by name, who together can be highly influential to a lot of different groups of people. Focus your energy on understanding why people share, and on using that understanding to create products and content that will be shared by small groups of close friends. If you manage this, and people naturally share your content with their friends, then those friends will naturally share with their own friends. Your message can reach millions of people, passed on by their most trusted sources, and it will all still feel personal.

How a big airline became personal

It's not easy to think about communication with small independent groups when you are big. One of the first big companies to do this successfully was KLM in November 2010, with an activity called KLM Surprise. The airline launched the experiment to see how happiness spreads when a few airline staff went out of their way to prepare gifts for passengers who had tweeted about their pending departure on a KLM flight. They saw a genuine smile of surprise on passengers' faces when KLM flight attendants greeted passengers by name as they arrived at security checkpoints and gates, and gave them a personalized gift.

KLM began by making it a priority to seek out their followers and build relationships with them. They created a website and Twitter feed dedicated to their campaign, joined Foursquare, and posted the video on their YouTube channel and the KLM Facebook page. They wanted to start and join conversations on those platforms, and get a feel for what their customers are really like.

They then took it one step further and personalized their campaign. They could have saved time and presented these passengers with a generic giveaway; instead, the employees took the time to learn more details, and give their customers something that had real value to them. KLM could have taken these insights into how to use social media further, but the idea and execution was impressive. They showed how to use digital media to ensure that a big enterprise is perceived as surprisingly human. A little research and little surprises earned them a million Twitter hits in one month as news of these surprises spread like wildfire through mentions, tweets, retweets and word of mouth (Peveto, 2011).

Critics, or brand ambassadors?

In this age of connectedness and transparency, customers don't hesitate to expose brands that provide bad customer service or product experiences. On the other hand, customers are also eager to share the great moments, the brand experiences that exceed their expectations. Proctor and Gamble call these 'blowing people away moments' (Neff, 2011), but they are also known as moments of surprise and delight or random acts of kindness. These acts of generosity have the power to raise the spirits of individuals or groups and raise perception of the brand in their minds.

Going that extra mile, and making the effort to personally surprise customers, stems from the knowledge that each satisfied customer can reach hundreds or thousands of potential future customers through social media. Just as you love to tell the story of the restaurant that gave you a complementary bottle of champagne on your anniversary, or free cake on your birthday, these moments inspire you to share the stories of brand goodwill with friends and family.

Many brands now leverage such surprise and delight moments to build positive word-of-mouth with existing and potential customers. KLM was one of the first, but they are far from the last.

Coca Cola's 'Happiness is Home' project brings happiness to a few of the 11 million Filipinos working overseas, when the brand brings them home for the holidays (Coca Cola, 2012). Tropicana created a large, inflated, glowing 'sun' during the dark, Arctic month-long polar night as part of their new 'Brighter Mornings for Brighter Days' campaign (Marketwire, 2010). And Spanair's 'Luggage Surprise' moment surprised customers who had to fly late on Christmas Eve with presents on the luggage carousel while they waited for their bags (Spanair, 2010). These feel-good moments generate a warm feeling both for the people who are part of the moment and for those who watch a video of it later.

What led to these socially driven moments of surprise and delight?

A number of factors contribute to today's use of surprise and delight moments. As trust in brands and corporations diminishes, people grow suspicious of brand promises and traditional transaction brand advertising.

The perception of businesses has become one of distant, inflexible, greedy corporations. In order to counteract this, brands need to create 'acts' instead of 'ads'. Actions speak louder than words and create valuable social and shareable connections.

Also, in today's social media-driven world, many people use social media platforms as an acceptable outlet to complain about everything from minor inconveniences to major life disruptions. This personal information, publically shared, offers brand owners valuable details about the lives, feelings and locations of their customers. With the help of these details, brands can identify, follow and communicate with existing and potential customers.

Unlike with traditional customer and loyalty rewards, these surprise and delight moments do not merely reward the customer for liking a brand on Facebook, or tweeting about it. Instead, these random acts of kindness aim to surprise the customer when they least expect it. It is the spontaneous conversations and mentions that offer the most value: customers talking about and sharing these moments on social media platforms.

How do brands benefit?

The first, and most obvious, benefit is simple word-of-mouth advertising. This has long been seen as the best form of advertising a brand can have, and with the massive potential reach each of your customers has through social media, the value of word-of-mouth has increased immensely. Brands can also leverage the content to create and maintain conversations with their customers and users. One of the key reasons that new videos go viral is the moment of pleasant surprise that viewers experience.

Surprisingly human brands capture the interest of informed consumers looking for brands with a similar belief and value system to their own. Through acts of generosity, compassion and humanity a brand can create a persona brand affinity that people identify with and want to be a part of.

How brands can get involved

When creating moments of surprise, brands need to let their brand code guide them. The surprise must be contextually relevant to their customers and visibly connected to their brand purpose and values. In this way, the moment of surprise reinforces the brand's position in people's minds and builds a positive connection that can influence later decision making.

Vincent Teo, an author for the digital marketing information site Clickz. com, identified three great social media brand examples (Teo, 2012):

- Edge Shave Gel built on the functional promise of preventing irritation after shaving. They sought out users who complained about everyday irritations on Twitter and helped relieve these irritations by sending humorous replies and gifts of everything from breakfast cereals to computers.

- Female sanitary brand Kotex created a great campaign in which they invented Women's Inspiration Day as a way of celebrating each woman as an individual. Because Pinterest is a social media platform dedicated to being a source of inspiration, Kotex searched the platform and reached out to 50 inspiring women. They then looked closely at each woman's Pinterest board to discover what inspired them and created personally decorated packages filled with things the women wanted.

- Kleenex tied their surprise moment with their brand purpose by reaching out to people who had listed Facebook status updates that announced they were not feeling well. Kleenex sent out special Kleenex kits to help them recover.

Why do some messages go viral and not others?

In a research paper called 'What makes online content viral?', Jonah Berger and Katherine Milkman show how surprise is one of the most important requirements of content, after practical value and interest (Berger and Milkman, 2012). Practical value and interest are usually addressed at the product innovation and development stage, but surprise can be effectively used later on, as well.

Another study by the CEO of NeuroBusiness, Srini Pillay M.D., showed that we can, in fact, predict which messages will go viral and which messages won't. Ideas that spread out have a distinct, recognisable characteristic that lies, surprisingly, in the brain of the sender. Messages that spread trigger two key areas in the sender's brain. The first of these registers rewards, the value that the sender places on the message. The second area deals with the ability to see things from the message receiver's point of view (Pillay, 2014).

When we, as brand managers, create our message, it is these two factors that help determine whether the message will go viral or not. The more you value an idea, and the more accurately you can predict how others will perceive the message, the more successful you will be at spreading it.

The smartphone and relation brand media

We make history every second. Today, two billion people have the most powerful, personal piece of technology ever built: the smartphone mobile device (Mawston, 2015). And with it comes access to sets of different apps for different purposes and tasks in our lives.

Our mobile devices and apps have become the media through which we relate to almost everything in our lives. They have become our true and trusted tech friends, accompanying us on our voyage through life, connecting us every day not only with people, but also with most of the services and product brands we use, both online and offline. Few people buy a car today without using the internet, whether it's to find information that helps you decide which model to buy, or finding the dealer you want to buy from. And inside the car, the in-built mobile device is a central part of the car product. Today, your car is usually connected to the web through GSM, with integrated navigation, communication and information systems. In recent years, I have met several people who decide which car to buy based mostly on whether they like the car's devices and software.

In 1964 the Canadian media philosopher Marshall McLuhan coined in the expression 'the media is the message' in his book, *Understanding Media: The extensions of man* (McLuhan, 1964). He meant that the technology and medium itself had developed a greater impact than the information you were trying to communicate through it. As a branding thinker, educator and advisor, I am similarly impressed by the branding impact of mobile apps. Thus, I am bound to piggy-back on McLuhan and coin the phrase 'the app is the brand'.

As noted in Chapter 9, the interactive app is the third generation of brand window, after the first generation packaged branded product and the second generation of advertising. Because the app is so completely integrated with the customer, the brand and product then the app, whatever the device (iPad, tablet, iWatch or built in to a piece of eyewear), becomes the brand. And not only in the eyes of the beholder, but also in the mind and the touch of the beholder-who-is-also-user, over and over again.

That is the whole point: we are directly involved with our apps. They are an essential part of how we manage our lives. They question our intelligence when we fill in forms. They challenge our performance when we exercise. They advise us like friends, offering suggestions on where to go to eat, shop and entertain ourselves. Our apps are part of our own self-identity. They are even part of our own attempt to be, or become, a personal brand ourselves.

Many of us have a lot of apps on our phones that we never use. This is another important thing for the app creators; your apps have to be the most liked, and the most used, too!

Conclusion: Social media apps are the key to building relation brands and creating customer experience

It is more important than ever that brands and businesses regain trust and attention by becoming more personal and more individualized. Relation brands have to master the personal conversations.

It is especially important for big organizations to become part of personal conversations within many smaller groups of people, and to break the patterns of one-way communication to make these conversations unexpected and interesting enough for participants to share with other people they are emotionally close to, thereby re-creating trust and credibility for the brands. Smartphone apps can be excellent channels for individuals to communicate directly with their brands, but only if the app is relevant, provides a good user experience and creates value for today's demanding users.

References

Berger, J and Milkman, K (2012) What makes online content viral?, *Journal of Marketing Research*, April, **49** (2), pp 192–205

Coca Cola (2012) Sweetest reunion video ever from the 'Happiness Is Home' project. [Video, online] www.coca-colacompany.com/ [Last accessed: 26.2.16]

Dunbar, R *et al* (2013) Social laughter is correlated with an elevated pain threshold, *PubMed*. [Online] http://www.ncbi.nlm.nih.gov/pubmed/21920973 [Last accessed: 26.2.16]

Fogg, BJ (2003) *Persuasive Technology: Using computers to change what we think and do*, Morgan-Kaufmann, San Francisco

Marketwired (2010) Canada's juice leader to become national provider of 'Brighter Mornings for Brighter Days', *Marketwired*, 26 Februrary. [Online] www.marketwired.com [Last accessed: 26.2.16]

Mawston, N (2015) Two billion people worldwide now own a smartphone, *Strategy Analytics*, 26 February. [Online] www.strategyanalytics.com [Last accessed: 26.2.16]

McLuhan, M (1964) *Understanding Media: The extensions of man*, McGraw-Hill, New York

Neff, J (2011) P&G: Moments that blow people away, *Ad Age*, **82** (7, February)

Peveto, A (2011) KLM surprise: How a little research earned 1,000,000 impressions on Twitter. [Online] www.digett.com [Last accessed: 20.1.16]

Pillay, S (2014) Which messages go viral and which ones don't? *Harvard Business Review*. [Online] https://hbr.org/2014/04/which-messages-go-viral-and-which-ones-dont [Last accessed: 20.1.16]

Boase, J, Horrigan, JB, Wellman, B and Raine, L (2006) *The Strength of Internet Ties*, PewResearchCenter, 25 January. [Online] http://www.pewinternet.org/files/old-media/Files/Reports/2006/PIP_Internet_ties.pdf.pdf [Last accessed: 15.1.16]

Spanair (2010) Spanair – unexpected luggage [Video, online] www.youtube.com/ [Last accessed: 26.2.16]

Teo, V (2012) Creating brand advocacy through surprise and delight moments, Clickz. [Online] www.clickz.com [Last accessed: 20.1.16]

Crisis brand management through surprise　13

Breaking a bad pattern in an unexpected way

When working as a brand adviser, if you are not the very first one who is called upon in a crisis you will be the second. Over the years I have been urgently contacted many times to help fix bad branding situations, and have gained considerable experience on the branding aspects of crisis situations. These aspects essentially cover the quick management of the perception and reputation of the company in crisis.

There are, of course, other considerations in a crisis situation, such as technical, supplier, organisational, financial or shareholder issues or government relations that are possibly equally important. But these are usually easier to handle than the branding-related topics, which concern what happens in people's minds. Often the vacuum of information in the beginning of a crisis situation creates a space of speculation and pure fantasy about what has happened. And people usually perceive that whatever happened will affect the brand badly.

Most serious crises arise when something inside the company, like a bad behaviour pattern that has been allowed to take root in the organisation, finally becomes public. Outdated and obsolete company cultures, or insensitive and wrong individual behaviours that have been accepted can consciously or subconsciously destroy honesty, ethics or transparency – the very core of company and brand culture.

Volkswagen's emission manipulation, 2015

We saw one example of such a crisis in 2015, when the top management of Volkswagen Group allowed the manipulation of emission performance results. The testing of close to 10 million diesel cars was shown to have systematically faked results by using software programmed to display lower emissions (Hotten, 2015). This led to a major catastrophe. The financial setback for the entire Volkswagen Group could have massive; share values initially plummeted, with both the Volkswagen and Audi brands directly affected.

In the wake of the scandal I was asked by journalists and business leaders if the company would survive this. My answer was always the same: yes, of course. The reason why I felt so sure of this is that the scandal never affected the customer. On the contrary, because of the environmental deceptions most of the customers' cars actually performed better than they should have from a horsepower and fuel economy standpoint (Karp and Yerek, 2015). The only negative effect on customers was the surprise after the fact that their cars were now going to be taken in for repairs that would ensure they met environmental standards, and that they might not be as good to drive afterwards. A more direct harm to the customers would have been a worse scenario for Volkswagen.

However, while many top automotive brands have suffered crises almost as large and dangerous, with non-functioning breaks and similar near-fatal flaws, most have survived. Of greater concern than Volkswagen's own survival is that the repercussions extend to the entire German car industry, and even trust in German industry in general. Comments such as, 'this could happen anywhere in the world, but not in Germany,' were typical. The long-term effect on Brand Germany is hard to estimate, if it is possible at all.

Amazingly, while sales of Volkswagen's namesake brand fell in the months following the scandal, in spite of industry-wide increases in sales, the Volkswagen Group's market share had already begun to rise again in January 2016, just three months after the scandal broke (Lavell, 2016).

Journalists and business leaders also asked me what could be done to make the brand recover. My suggestion was to break the pattern of a macho men's club at Volkswagen and exchange the very top management with a woman CEO. Mostly my suggestion came from a desire to surprisingly break the pattern, but such an act would also be perceived as introducing a more environmental and people-caring company culture to broaden the horizons and prepare the Volkswagen Group for the challenges of tomorrow. With global warming, strict emission control and the role of private vehicles in the practical lives of the people of our planet taking more space in the discussion, I felt that more women in the car industry could bring great benefits to this boys' toys business.

How 'United breaks guitars' broke a pattern of not listening to customers' complaints

Today, we see another type of crisis in business as well. Rather than beginning collectively with thousands of people making thousands of complaints and claims, these new crises involve individual neglected claims that would have gone unheard in the past. Despite the difference in scope, these individual claims crises can be almost as harmful. In today's interconnected world, they have the potential to quickly develop into crisis situations that reach millions of others, and inspire them to air their own emotions and grievances. What you then see is a snowball effect, with one triggering event bringing out more relevant personal scandals and adding them to the pile, making a large fire out of what seemed to be a very small one.

The reason these small claims can escalate is, of course, social media and the unbelievable and surprising power it grants individuals. Social media breaks patterns and surprises us over and again with each new revelation of how much power we all actually have when it comes to turning things upside down.

An early crisis in this individual claims category is 'United breaks guitars'. It started with Dave Carroll, a Canadian musician that most people had never heard of. Together with his band, Dave created a YouTube video chronicle of his real-life experience of how his fine guitar was broken during a trip on United Airlines in 2008, and the subsequent reaction from the airline. The song was released in July 2009 and became an immediate YouTube and iTunes hit. It also became a public relations embarrassment for the airline. In the song, Dave Carroll relates how his guitar was broken while in United Airlines' custody. He alleged that a fellow passenger exclaimed that baggage handlers on the tarmac at Chicago's O'Hare Airport were throwing guitars during a layover on his flight, and when he arrived at his destination he discovered that his $3,500 Taylor guitar was severely damaged. The lyrics of the song include the line: 'I should have flown with someone else, or gone by car, 'cause United breaks guitars' (Carroll, 2009).

The YouTube video was posted on 6 July 2009 and with its first day it had amassed 150,000 views. It reached one million views after only one month, and five million after just over two months. This massive exposure prompted United to contact Carroll and offer to right the wrong. Within four days of the video being posted online, United Airlines' stock price fell 10 per cent, costing stockholders about $180 million in value (Ayres, 2009).

Since the incident, Carroll has been in great demand as a speaker on customer service, and ironically, on one of his trips as a speaker, United Airlines lost his luggage. The song was named one of the top 10 viral videos of 2009 by *Time* magazine (Fletcher, 2009) and even featured on a CBC/CNBC documentary called *Customer (Dis)Service*.

In May 2012 Carroll published a book detailing his experiences: *United Breaks Guitars: The power of one voice in the age of social media* (Carroll, 2012). Time after time, the success of Carroll's online protest has been used exemplify a new kind of threat that corporations face in the internet age and held up as an example of a good way to complain while remaining respectful, without yelling.

How Greenpeace and Norsk Hydro changed the PVC industry

When the workers of the Norsk Hydro PVC plant in Stenungsund on the west coast of Sweden came to work in the early morning one day in 1996, a young man in an orange overall was chained to the factory gates as though crucified. Journalists and TV crews were already in place. This was just one of many actions that Greenpeace took during that year to fight the usage of chlorine and other toxins in the manufacturing of PVC. This plastic material is widely used in many industries and high on Greenpeace's list was its use in packaging, building, the automotive industry and medical applications. Because of the dioxin released when PVC is incinerated or burned, Greenpeace wanted to ensure that the highly profitable plant would be closed.

The factory management quickly produced a full page of text in the regional newspaper, *GT*, where they tried to explain that PVC is not at all dangerous when treated correctly. Unfortunately, they used a lot of words to say very little and, as Greenpeace had hoped, Norsk Hydro's effort just made things worse. Instead of a well-reasoned and informative explanation, their response looked exactly like typical cold-hearted and cynical industrialists desperately trying to defend themselves.

I was called in as a branding and communications consultant to help the Norsk Hydro management team. The first thing I did was to explain to them how communication works. I felt that this seemingly obvious step was necessary because most of the management team was made up of engineers and business administrators who had never needed to know how to manage perceptions in people's minds. I began by sketching out a universal communication model (Figure 13.1).

I suggested that instead of continuing to do what everyone expected them to do – explain with facts – Norsk Hydro should do the opposite and actually attack Greenpeace using their own methods. Instead of reacting and defending, they could break both their own expected pattern and the pattern of the common view on plastics as something we just use and carelessly throw away: waste without value.

I had two ideas on how they could break this pattern of perception in people's minds, about plastic in general and PVC in particular.

The first idea grew serendipitously from a meeting I'd had a few weeks earlier with a Swedish artist called Carouschka. She had told me that she wanted to create an exhibition about plastics inspired by a huge collection of everyday plastic items that a Stockholm advertising art director has

Figure 13.1 The universal communication model

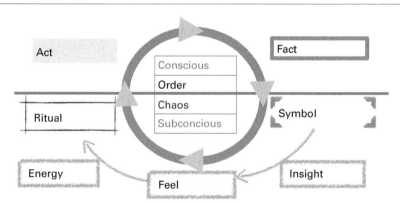

Communication usually starts as the frustrating illusion of turning *fact* to *act* inside the closed domain of order and conscious thinking, but this never succeeds since facts lack emotional energy and in order to become a successful communicator one always has to charge the message with *feeling*. This is created by finding an emotional link in the message with help of *symbol and myth*. Now emotional *energy* is created and takes the form of symbolic action, also called *ritual*, to power people's minds and make them *act*. And after actions there is always a genuine interest in the *facts* to explain, structure and manifest what just happened. And so all good communication continues successfully in a spiral, a repeating circle movement upwards, lifted by new *insight* with every full circle.

accumulated. Carouschka wanted to add to his collection and create a major plastics display at the most visible cultural venue right in the heart of Stockholm, Kulturhuset. However, financing was an issue.

Therefore, I asked Norsk Hydro if they would consider funding it, pointing out the opportunity of breaking the pattern of what Norsk Hydro, plastic and PVC stood for at that moment in time. They agreed and within a month the exhibition was successfully launched. It gathered a lot of attention from the media and culturally influential people within Sweden and prompted one of the top cultural journalists to write the headline 'Plastic – the modern gold' in his review of the exhibition. In one stroke of the media, plastic was transformed into something with cultural and artistic value. And the centrepiece of the exhibition was a plastic bag containing blood, hanging from its hook and ready to deliver a life-saving blood infusion to a model human arm. Despite the toxins emitted when waste PVC is incinerated, its use is invaluable in medicine and it is the only material that can contain blood without risk of contagion.

The second activity I suggested also worked towards the goal of supporting a sense of value instead of waste. This activity was to immediately start a recycling programme for plastics in Sweden. Convincing the engineers and economists in the management team to do this was a tough proposition for two reasons. First, the art exhibition was much easier to buy into, because there was already a plan in place that simply needed to be put into action. A recycling programme would need to be built from nothing. The second reason was that the recycling of plastics was technically difficult to manage and was not considered economical. I had to turn to the universal communication model once again to explain that the recycling had nothing to do with making money, nor did it even need to carry its own cost. Instead, it was symbolically essential to help people perceive plastic as something with its own value, as opposed to something worthless that you just throw away when you're done with it.

The amazing and unexpected result of all this was a kind of truce that developed between Norsk Hydro and Greenpeace. It became the story of how non-profit organizations like Greenpeace, who had initially lobbied for a total European Union ban on PVC, had a serious impact on commercial companies like Norsk Hydro (Hadler, 2013). This impact created a game-changing effect in the PVC business that began in Sweden and quickly spread around the world. It fundamentally changed the industry's approach and launched the drive to develop a sustainable business strategy and the development of PVC manufacturing techniques that replaced the toxic and poisonous ingredients with stabilized and non-toxic alternatives.

Conclusion: Crises are important brand issues to be solved by breaking expected patterns

We have very clear, stereotyped expectations about how an industry should act in crises: first with silence, followed by denial, attempts to explanation or threats. Simply breaking that expected pattern creates the possibility for you to find your way out of the crisis with the respect of your opponents and with limited damage. It's not enough today to turn around and admit a mistake. Now, you have to offer good reasons that explain your past choices and find a way to repair the damage caused by corporate mistakes. Which in turn are usually caused by the wrong corporate culture. As with the Norsk Hydro case, it may even be possible to turn a crisis into an acclaimed success by bringing people together.

References

Ayres, C (2009) Revenge is best served cold – on YouTube, *The Times*, 22 July. [Online] www.thetimes.co.uk [Last accessed: 20.2.16]

Carroll, D (2009) United breaks guitars [Video, online] www.youtube.com [Last accessed: 25.2.16]

Carroll, D (2012) *United Breaks Guitars: The power of one voice in the age of social media*, Hay House, Inc, New York

Fletcher, D (2009) Top 10 viral videos, *Time* Magazine, 8 December, Available from: www.time.com [Last accessed: 20.2.16]

Hadler, T (2013) Transform conflict into collaboration, Network for Business Sustainability, 25 November. [Online] nbs.net/knowledge/ [Last accessed: 26.2.16]

Hotten, R (2015) Volkswagen: The scandal explained, BBC News, 10 December. [Online] www.bbc.com/ [Last accessed: 25.2.16]

Karp, G and Yarek, B (2015) Volkswagen owners should be nervous about emissions scandal, experts say, *Chicago Tribune*, 22 September. [Online] my.chicagotribune.com [Last accessed: 25.2.16]

Lavell, T (2016) VW loses European market share to Fiat in wake of scandal, Bloomberg Business, 16 February. [Online] www.bloomberg.com [Last accessed: 25.2.16]

Company
surprise culture

14

Making your employees feel special

The company culture is very much the same thing as a brand. If a company is to create great customer experience and surprises, it obviously has to be supported by the culture within the company. There are many examples of how very different and surprising company cultures are the real sources of business success. This is especially true in business categories that are less exciting, even boring, or not known for creating any anticipations of surprise.

One amazing example of business success that sprang from the culture introduced by its founder, Jack Ma, is Alibaba, an e-commerce company that provides a variety of sales services via web portals. You can read many examples on the internet of how this works for Jack Ma, from the huge party events with him clowning as a front figure and living up to one of his core business principles, 'Take your business but not yourself seriously' (Zakkour, 2014), to the mass weddings he arranges. Every year, he invites all newly married couples in his large organization to a 'mass wedding' – a huge event celebrating their marriages. Of course, the people in his organization love their crazy boss. They feel special just working for him.

Jack Ma's charismatic leadership has created an organization filled with people who look up to him as a role model and an example of success. The facts that he was a school teacher of English, that he started his business in his kitchen, that it developed into one of the biggest businesses on the internet, and in the world, and that he himself became one of the world's wealthiest individuals, embody the cultural and brand message implicit in nearly everything he says: 'everything is possible, and you can do everything you want. It's up to you'.

Another famous example is Zappos, which began as an online shoe retailer. In a business category that is seldom perceived as cool or advanced, the only differentiation between Zappos and millions of similar businesses was the company culture. CEO Tony Hsieh maintains a slightly weird company culture, where one of the 10 core values is to create fun and a little weirdness. Being a little weird is held as an important trait for getting hired in the first place. After training, employees have been paid to leave not because they under-performed, but because they do not fit into the company culture (*Harvard Business Review*, 2008). Zappos is now an independent part of Amazon after Amazon acquired it for one billion dollars in July, 2009 – amazing money even for a company with a sensational customer experience record.

A third example of strong and effective brand culture is the Swedish company, IKEA, the world retail leader in furniture and items for the home. What is surprising when compared to many other international business cultures is the Swedish management style that is an integrated part of the brand culture of IKEA.

The IKEA company management culture is best described by a Chinese employee of IKEA, Angela Zhu, manager of an IKEA Store in Shanghai:

> The team approach at IKEA that we have, with no hierarchy, is very much appreciated. It is a challenge, however, to make sure everyone is certain of their responsibility. We have to assume responsibility. Some of our co-workers and professionals have worked in other foreign-owned stores, such as B&Q, Carrefour and Wal-Mart. They see a big difference. Here, they feel it is OK to act. When we hire new people, we do it by means of value-based recruiting. We set very clearly our vision and values – straightforwardness, being humble and taking the initiative. Being humble is nothing new in China, but the way we do it at Ikea is to express our strong desire and initiative in a humble way.
>
> (Isaksson. 2008)

How to build an excellent customer experience culture

Sometimes, I find entrepreneurs are more interested in culture than branding, until I tell them it's the same. Then, they become motivated to bring branding in at an earlier stage. While most people who are not in the business of branding assume that branding is closely tied to marketing, the truth is that the company culture is basically the same as the brand. Or at least, company culture is a very close application of the brand fundamentals.

There are five fundamental insights that help you use a strong, differentiated, internal company culture to build your customer experience branding.

1 **Make your people feel free.** When your people feel free within, yet at the same time personally dependent on, your company culture, they will never want to leave you for another job, not even for a better paid one. You should offer a top, attractive workplace that they can be proud of.

2 **Create a surprising and unexpected culture.** The surprising experiences spring out of the founder's personal, authentic, crazy ideas or views on life. The purpose is to make it different from other workplaces. Working for a company that dares to be different makes you feel different, and that is the whole point. People today can do a job similar to other jobs, and live a life similar to other people's lives, but if they work in a place with a strong and different culture, they will feel different.

3 **Keep the feeling of difference alive.** Ritual events led by the founders, like Jack Ma's annual 'mass weddings', make the people who work for that founder feel personally connected. And that perceived closeness, or identification, is the backbone of a strong company culture.

4 **Build a strong company brand and culture for no other reason than to make it an attractive place to work.** If the brand attracts people who want to work with you, the salary level is secondary, the career possibilities are secondary, even work satisfaction is secondary. Being a cool place to work, with a strong internal culture, holds great value for branding and marketing the company and its products in today's relation branding context.

5 **Start or strengthen your culture with a good 'why'.** As Simon Sinek put it in his book (Sinek, 2009), 'Any organization can explain *what* it does, some can explain *how* they do it; but very few can clearly articulate *why*'. The biggest mistake a leader can make is to tell us that we should work to achieve revenue, or a profit. The why, the reason, is not money or profit. Money and profit are the results. You need to know your 'noble cause' – why your organization exists and why your project is important.

Examples of noble causes

These are some examples of slogans that express the *why* (or the noble cause) of brands:

'Building a better world through the power of design' – Rhode Island School of Design

'We renew life' – Amgen

'Everybody's got a win' – NASCAR

'We are about organizing federal employees to ensure that each federal employee is treated with dignity and respect' – National Treasury Employees Union

'A world of play and interconnection for everyone' – Explorati

'Creating opportunities for all athletes' – Special Olympics

'To make information available to everybody in the world' – Google

'To make a contribution to the world by making tools for the mind that advance humankind' – Apple

'Delivering happiness to customers, employees and vendors' – Zappos

'Increasing the effectiveness and enhancing the lives of CEOs' – Vista International

How SAS took off again with their most important passengers on board

At the turn of the 21st century, Scandinavia's top advertising agencies were invited to pitch for the most prestigious advertising account in Scandinavia: Scandinavian Airline Systems (SAS). One of Europe's oldest airlines, SAS is owned to a large extent by the governments of Norway, Sweden and Denmark.

The pitch took half a year and I was the Scandinavian Creative Director of the winning agency, leading three advertising teams in each of the three countries. However, when we met with the SAS representatives for a briefing on the adverting we expected to start soon, we received a shock. Between the airline and its customers lay a barrier of total distrust. The situation was so serious that if there been any good alternative for the customers, most of them would have left and chosen to go with someone else. As it was, despite the recent appearance of low-cost carriers, SAS held a virtual monopoly on most routes in 2000; there was no practical alternative.

In describing the situation, our new client informed us that it simply couldn't do any advertising until it dealt with the customers' complaints and improve the bad service experience. SAS believed that its customers would only react with anger if SAS began a new advertising campaign at that time.

We were an advertising team and as we returned despondently to the agency that afternoon, I remember thinking about only one thing: how to get around the advertising ban. How could we start changing the perception about the airline in the minds of their customers without advertising, and create a trust on which we could build a come-back, change the service and later create ads to support that process?

The key lay in breaking the pattern that everyone, both internally and externally, experienced with SAS. The company culture was perceived to be retiring. It had lost the charisma it had been known for under a previous CEO, Jan Carlzon, who successfully transformed SAS into 'The Businessman's Airline' by promoting the status of business class. Despite the flatter social class structure in Scandinavia, this focus remained successful until deregulation and the emergence of new competitors began to water down the business class service model. In his book, he explains how he rebuilt the corporate culture to encourage taking decisions at lower levels, making the organization flatter, decentralized and more effective (Carlzon, 1989). It was a fantastic backdrop for a new change. The internal culture was already in place, ready to use for a second change programme, this time making it even more inclusive.

My idea was to rewind this old clock, energize it and break it out of its patterns by involving everyone. Beginning internally at first, and then developing external involvement by bringing in the airline customers, we literally bring them on board to help to change the airline. This was the first time I really understood the power of inclusion, the power that comes when both staff and customer participate, working together and committing to success. We brought everyone on board, with no one left complaining on the ground.

I learned another important lesson at that time as well: when your customers are furious at you and complaining loudly about your bad service, you still have a chance for your business to survive. It's when your customers are quiet and silently turn their backs on you that you should be terrified and close down your business as soon as you can to stop the money drain. When people complain, they are still interested in you and still hope to see you improve and break out of the crisis. While you still hold the interest of your customers, even if they are forced to be interested in you because they have no alternatives, they are still interested in helping you recover. In fact, they want you to use them as advisors. The want you listen to them and give them the chance to participate in whatever small capacity they can. It is important that your customers feel that they are important to you and that you respect them as customers. When they feel that, they begin to respect you and believe that you can change your business to become better for them.

So, since we had been told we could not advertise, I decided to carry out a major research project instead. My own teams thought I was crazy – we were an advertising agency, not a research agency – but nevertheless, we asked our client if we could bring in some management consultants to sweep through the entire organization and find out what ideas the internal staff had for service development and improvement.

Since all lasting change begins internally through building confidence within the people inside the organization, this proved to be a very successful idea (see Chapter 15 for more information on this). Our massive survey resulted in a catalogue of over 100 change projects covering everything from ticketless travel to new uniforms to new food on board to new lounges. It also included some obvious solutions like modern aircraft and excellent timekeeping.

From this list, we chose 90 projects and recommended that our client ask their real frequent flyers what they thought about each of them. These 250,000 Gold Members were the people who truly kept the airline in the air. The rest of the 10 million passengers who filled the planes contributed only marginally to the business. Our client was reluctant at first. Understandably, they didn't want to irritate their already complaining core customers further by asking them 90 questions, even if they only asked for answers on a scale of 1 to 5. Their frequent flyers were business people, important and busy people whose time was too valuable to waste on lengthy surveys. Or so SAS believed. Fortunately, we were able to convince them that it was a matter of perception. A survey of only 30 questions would not be perceived as serious. A survey of 90 questions clearly took time and effort to prepare and implied that we had already invested enough in it to really be interested in the answers.

SAS gave us the permission we needed and we had a 95 per cent answer rate. Almost all of the busy frequent business travellers wanted to participate in making a change. They expected a change in the service. They expected improvement and believed that SAS could do it, and this gave the airline a tremendous boost to its internal self-confidence and increased its ability to perform better.

When we were finally able to return to our work as an advertising agency, we began with advertising in smaller formats to test the waters. Despite our clients' fears, no one responded in anger at all, even though most of the improvements had not yet been made. But every ad was functional. Each ad described the improvement of a new service or product, introducing each improvement one by one. The ads were equipped with a 'meter-box' that displayed how many of the experienced business travellers had voted for and highly evaluated this particular improvement in our survey.

What was even more amazing was that, in our follow-up interviews, customers told us they felt that they had really participated in bringing the airline back on track, flying straight and smooth again and successful. The recovery in general customer experience kicked in quicker than expected; after only half a year, big changes occurred in the attitudes of passengers. The final step in turning around the airline was the packaging of all the improvements by a good design firm. A fresh corporate identity was launched with new aircraft livery, new uniforms and a new lounge design.

The re-design was developed under the brand idea 'It's Scandinavian'. The airline looked smarter, more modern, more Scandinavian and the staff stood tall and once again became 'The Businessman's Airline' that had all but collapsed 10 years earlier, proud of themselves. And their customers were happy and back on board.

Conclusion: Company culture is branding, and inclusion is the name of the game

SAS was able to turn its failing customer service experience around by including both its staff and its customers in the repair project and making everyone feel special. By asking people, internally and externally, what they want and how they would improve your company, you show them the highest respect and they, in turn, will respect you.

For this reason, it is important that your company is well organized and not too bureaucratic. It's important to hire good people who can produce results, people with a little independence who are not easy to lead and who are a little bit crazy. This personalization of the corporate culture, this emphasis on 'culture' and de-emphasis on 'corporate', is important in bringing out people's capacity to motivate themselves and lead themselves.

A culture of surprise starts internally and spreads externally to customers, partners and suppliers. Therefore, it is important that the leadership creates positive surprises for the people working in a company, whether it is by being crazy or simply asking for help when the culture has become depressed and stagnant because of crises.

Finally, inclusion by definition creates a cooperative culture in which staff and customers feel that they are working together for the benefit of all. We are social beings and we need companies to include a social context. Where we work defines who we are. And while the social context will always be a reason for people to work for larger organizations, they do have to understand and cultivate their own culture and their own self-confidence.

References

Carlzon, J (1989) *Moments of Truth: New strategies for today's customer-driven economy*, HarperBusiness, New York

Harvard Business Review (2008) Why Zappos pays new employees to quit – And you should too. [Video, online] www.youtube.com [Last accessed: 25.2.16]

Isaksson, P (2008) *Leading Companies in a Global Age: Managing the Swedish way*, Vinnova report VR 2008:14, Vinnova

Sinek, S (2009) *Start with Why: How great leaders inspire everyone to take action*, Portfolio Hardcover, New York

Zakkour, M (2014) How Jack Ma's 'crazy' management style built a technology empire, *Entrepreneur*, 29 September. [Online] www.entrepreneur.com/ [Last accessed: 25.2.16]

The surprising power of individuals 15

How self-confidence drives customer experience

We live in the generation of the selfie. At no point in history have we been so focused on our own individual differences and self-actualization. As an employer, this has become a problem. How do you inspire people to perform, even with jobs that do not particularly promote self-actualization?

Another important aspect of this focus on individualism within today's businesses is creating the organization's self-confidence to continually disrupt and surprise. Some say it is all about motivation and financial rewards. Others (fewer today than in previous decades) believe that punishing those who don't perform is more effective.

It truth, company self-confidence stems mainly from the self-actualization and self-confidence of the key employees. In some companies, this group includes every employee at the company.

What do customers appreciate most in the best customer experience brands?

Individual employees who interact with customers become a proxy for the brand. If they demonstrate the wrong behaviours the damage can be hugely expensive, but getting them right does not cost a huge amount of money. Most often, good customer experience is a function of the positive, helpful attitude of the individual.

Over the years, I have asked people who work in companies with very good customer experience brands what they consider to be the most important and most appreciated individual characteristics. The same answers keep coming up. We perceive a good customer experience when we interact with people who are courteous and friendly, people who listen to us and are interested in us, and people who are genuine, happy and not pushy.

Perhaps surprisingly, we are often less impressed by how knowledgeable an individual is, and more impressed by how positive they are and how proactive they are in looking for a solution. People who respect their colleagues and who are not afraid to ask for help often seem even more helpful than the person who recites all the answers. Being engaged, passionate and proud of the product or service is another attitude that shines through and is appreciated by customers.

It's easy to see how these qualities lead to a good customer experience. Each one of them focuses on paying attention and treating the customer with respect. And even if the customer has a problem that cannot ultimately be solved, being respected and knowing that an individual genuinely tried to help often leads to a positive customer experience anyway.

How do the best customer experience brands manage personalization?

We are all individuals and we like to be treated as such. Personalized customer service from real people we can relate to reinforces positive feelings we have towards the brand, and can reduce negative feelings. Brands that succeed in creating the best customer experiences usually make the effort to get the personalisation right.

By understanding needs, anticipating desires and being proactive in the customer experience, you can begin to build a firm foundation for a good customer experience. Show that you listen to your customers by acting on the information they give you and keeping them informed with relevant information. Interactions between customers and company employees should always be personal, never just another transaction; make a connection and take the time to know your customer. You should also try to make things easier for your customers by remaining flexible and adaptable. Allowing your customers to control the degree of personalisation, in terms of frequency and content, gives the customer a feeling of respect and self-confidence.

How to improve self-confidence

Simply being confident yourself helps the customers you interact with to feel confidence themselves. Yet, we have all experienced times of low self-confidence, and at those times it becomes much harder to provide the personalized customer experience we strive for.

While it often feels impossible to boost your self-confidence, I believe that we can all increase our self-confidence whenever we need to; you do not have to be reliant on others. No matter what it is that you temporarily believe – that you are not competent, not smart, not successful – you can change your perceptions. And you can do this by taking concrete actions.

The actions described below are not a definitive list of self-confidence boosting actions, and you do not need to do all of them or follow the same order I have laid them out here. Begin with one or just a few in combination, then try others. Some will work, some won't. Some work most of the time, but not always. Low self-confidence can be a tricky mind-set to change, and it takes time.

Take care of yourself

This simple act can turn your self-confidence around. It's amazing how much difference a shower can make in how you feel about yourself. Keep yourself well-groomed and dress comfortably in clothes you like and are happy to be seen in. When you can look at yourself in the mirror and nod in satisfaction, you'll find you feel successful, presentable and ready to face the challenges that await you.

Don't skimp on meals, or rush through them. You don't have to follow a strict diet or become a health and fitness guru, but taking the time to sit down and enjoy what you are eating goes a long way to reducing the stress that comes from feeling you are not good enough.

Improve your self-image

While taking care of yourself improves your outer image, to build true and lasting self-confidence you also need to improve your self-image. Our mental picture of ourselves defines our confidence, but it is not unchangeable. Visualization is a useful tool to use here. If there is something about yourself that you wish were different, take five minutes and visualize yourself acting as you want to act, being as you want to be. Our self-image is created by our thoughts and we can control those thoughts. Consciously thinking of positive images of yourself will, over time, improve your self-image.

Think positive

The power of conscious thought can also be used to train yourself to think positively all the time. Begin by taking some time every day just to be aware of your own thoughts. Linger on the positive thoughts and examine all the ways in which they positively affect your life. Don't ignore the negative thoughts, however. Instead, whenever they appear turn them around. Decide what the exact opposite, positive version of the negative thought is and focus on that. Treat it exactly as you treat the positive thoughts that come naturally and focus on how the positive version affects your life.

By turning negative thoughts into positive ones every time you notice them, you train yourself to think more positive thoughts, and positive thinking is one of the best self-confidence boosters I know of.

If you find it hard to think positive thoughts, a simple method to encourage them is simply to be grateful. Set aside 10 minutes each day to think of everything in your life that you are grateful for. If you can't think of anything, then be grateful for the simplest things. Be grateful that you are breathing. Be grateful that you have food and a roof over your head. Be grateful for your friends or even something that happened in the distant past. Make sure you use the full 10 minutes and concentrate on truly feeling grateful for a short while. In addition to helping you practise positive thinking, this simple exercise is a very positive self-confidence booster in itself.

Get to know yourself

When you take the time to focus on your thoughts, you inevitably learn a lot more about yourself than you knew before. It is not always a pleasant experience, but it is always useful. In order to solve any problem, you must first understand what the problem is. When the problem is a lack of self-confidence, what you need to understand is where that lack originates. Begin by keeping a journal about yourself and your thoughts about yourself. Analyse where the negative thoughts come from, and what you can do to eliminate or minimize the impact of that source. Analyse the positive thoughts, too, and find ways to encourage them. Consider your limitations and determine whether they are real or self-imposed. The ones you place on yourself can be turned into positive opportunities and the real limitations can be analysed to determine how limiting they really are. This action takes a lot of courage to dig deeply into yourself, but it can result in a huge increase of self-confidence in the end.

Act positive

While thinking positively has great benefits in itself, when you put those thoughts into positive actions you can multiply the effect. By changing what you do, you change who you are. Let your actions be positive: smile, be kind and generous, put energy into your actions. When you smile, you not only appear happy to others, but you trick your mind into believing you are happy, too.

Kind acts and generosity are huge self-confidence boosters not only for you, but for others as well. It allows you to feel good about yourself for a while and improves your self-image. And as I have previously said, improving self-image is itself a way to improve self-confidence.

Empower yourself

Empowering yourself is one of the best strategies for building self-confidence and it can be done in a number of different ways. One of the surest methods is increasing your knowledge. When you know more, you are more confident. So take the time to study something. Research topics that interest you, or that affect your life or business.

Increase your competence by practising what you have studied. Competency is another very successful way of empowering yourself. When you have learned something new, the only way to get better at it is to actually do it. You don't have to master everything at once; spend just 30 minutes each day practising it and your competency will steadily increase.

You can also empower yourself by being prepared. It's hard to be confident in yourself if you think you don't know enough, or haven't done enough. Preparing yourself as much as you can is a fairly straightforward way of increasing your self-confidence. If you are facing a speech, and don't believe you can talk in front of so many strangers, prepare yourself by giving your speech first to a mirror, and then to a close and supportive friend. Make sure all your notes, slides and props are prepared in advance and use them in your practices so you are fully prepared to use them in your speech.

Know your principles

If you don't know the principles that guide your life, you can feel that your life has no direction. It is hard to be confident when you are lost and don't know where you are going. Think hard about what your principle actually are and make sure that you do, in fact, live them. It's not enough to just say the words, they have to steer your actions as well.

Focus on solutions

If you find you are always complaining, or dwelling on the problems you encounter, you need to change that if you want to permanently boost your self-confidence. By focusing on solutions instead of problems, you break out of the sinking spiral that pulls your self-confidence down. Whenever a problem arises, think 'How can I solve that?' You might not be able to come up with a solution right away, but even if your first thought seems ridiculous take the time to seriously consider it before you discard it.

Set a small goal and achieve it

Nothing boosts self-confidence quite like success and you don't need to set ambitious goals to feel great about achieving them. It feels exactly the same when you set a goal you know you can achieve, and then achieve it.

Try to build a pattern of achieving goals. Set a small one. Achieve it. Then set another small goal and achieve that, too. In this way, you can achieve many goals in just one day. The more goals you reach, the better you'll feel and the more confident you'll be that you can set achievable goals. And the more confident you are about setting goals, the better you'll get at reaching them. Then you'll be able to set larger achievable goals and reach those as well.

Work on small things

The setting of small goals is a great way to break a big, unmanageable project into easy-to-complete sections. Instead of tackling a daunting and intimidating task, ask yourself what the first thing you need to do is and set that as your first goal. If you are creating a brand book, your first step might be to list the section headings. Then you can list the subheadings of the first section, followed by the subheadings of the third section.

The bigger and more complicated a project is, the smaller you can often make the individual steps. This has the double benefit of letting you work on small tasks while accumulating a series of successes as each task is completed. When you are judging your progress, don't look at how much you still have to work on. Look at your ever-growing list of everything you have done.

The actions outlined above are some of the most effective methods to increase self-confidence, but they are far from the only actions that work. Getting active and doing something you have been putting off for a while will almost always make you feel better about yourself. Exercise releases endorphins that reduce stress and trigger a positive feeling in the body. People who stand tall and speak slowly are often perceived as more confident than others and mimicking these actions can induce feelings of self-confidence. Even something as small as cleaning your desk can increase your self-confidence greatly.

And when your self-confidence is high, you can more easily inspire self-confidence in others.

Entrepreneurs' new interest in personal branding

One hundred years ago, the great industrialists like Henry Ford, Andrew Carnegie and Alfred Nobel inspired immense public interest. More recently, sports stars increased interest in their fields; Bjorn Borg inspired intense interest for tennis in many parts of the world, and Tiger Woods did the same for young aspiring golfers. Today public interest in business entrepreneurs, like Richard Branson, Elon Musk or Jeff Bezos, is greater than it has been at any time since the great industrialists built their businesses.

And this phenomenon of raising business entrepreneurs to role model status is of great importance in creating the interest these entrepreneurs, especially the younger ones, now show in branding. Becoming a role model is a well-known and highly appreciated path to becoming a leader in business and building the confidence and trust of a company.

At some, very early, point, you also have to care about how you build self-insight and self-confidence among all the individuals within your company. You not only need to co-brand yourself as the leader of your company brand, you also need to co-brand your people with your company. And that is exactly where personal branding can help. What follows is a brief, hands-on way to deal with the 'co-branding' situation between your brand and the brand of the company you founded or work for.

Create your 'brand me' strategy

Personal branding begins with identifying who you are. And you are the only expert on who you are. You only need some guidance along the way.

Companies can offer this as a very popular programme for their employees or you can do it on your own, with or without a personal guide.

In our version of personal branding, we start with coding your own personal brand, and we end with matching your personal brand with the company brand. Six steps take you from the beginning to the end:

1 **Base your personal brand on other people's views of who you are.** Send a form to your 10 most important friends, family members, job colleagues, clients or partners and ask them describe how they perceive your brand and reputation. This is similar to the 4-D method I described for company brands in Chapter 6.

2 **Start working on your own brand.** Before you read the 4-D brand-dimensions descriptions from your friends, family, colleagues and clients, define your own version of the four dimensions of your personal brand. When you have completed your version, compare it with your friends' versions. Use both your view and the views of others to determine what you might add or change in your final 'brand me' mind space, so that the result describes how you want yourself to become in other people's perceptions.

3 **Complete a 'brand me' code.** Following largely the same principles as described in Chapter 8 about coding your brand, create a 'brand me' motto for yourself.

4 **Test your 'brand me' code.** Use the 'brand me' activity generator to create activities in the four dimensions that can help you stretch out your personal brand in other people's perceptions, and make you significant and more interesting.

5 **Re-programme yourself.** If your personal brand is to be effective in changing your personality slightly, to become more like you want to be, you need to do one more thing: you need to go back in your mind to the major events in your life that will hold you back in the old tracks, and change those memories. It sounds difficult, but it is very doable with the help of a 'brand me' timeline. This neuro-linguistic programming technique is described in detail in the book *Managing Brand Me* (Gad and Rosencreutz, 2002).

6 **Synchronize your 'brand me' with your company brand.** Finally, in order to co-brand your own 'brand me' with your company brand, you need to create a brand for your company (or decode an existing brand). The method for doing this is detailed in this book (Chapters 6 and 8). Since the brand creation models are basically the same, this step is often easy. You can then study where your 'brand me' is synchronized with the company brand and where it is not.

Think about what these possible differences mean to you: conflicts, disagreements, different points of view, a company culture that is dissonant in a disturbing way. Evaluate how important this mismatch between the brands of your company and yourself is. If the difference is substantial, you might consider looking for another enterprise, or another place to work (and you decode and match their brand in the same way). When you are creating a company and a brand, the differences are usually small, the situation is more or less synchronized and everything is largely positive.

The insights you gain from following this process will strengthen the co-branding relationship between the company and your personal brand as the entrepreneur, founder or leader of the business. And it will make you aware of how you can use the synergies between the company brand and your own brand, to build and to mutually strengthen both brands.

Conclusion: It all boils down to self-confidence in individuals

Self-confidence within yourself, among your employees and among your customers is the key to creating a positive customer experience. A large organization is often measured in the area of customer experience by the performance of one individual. For this reason, it is of utmost importance to focus on the individuals in your organization and boost each individual's self-confidence. You can boost the self-confidence of others through your own self-confidence, which allows you to meet everyone with respect and competency. Boosting your own self-confidence can be done through the application of a number of concrete actions. Personal branding honours the individual and gives you space to work on your 'brand me' and how customers and colleagues perceive your personal performance.

In today's digital world of connected and therefore powerful individuals, individual behaviour becomes one of the most important determiners of whether your customer experience is good, or bad.

References

Gad, T and Rosencreutz, A (2002) *Managing Brand Me*, Momentum, WC2E Books, London

Case book

Some surprise cases

We all like to have a few solid cases before we truly accept any new structural idea, no matter how good the idea is. That goes for the concepts addressed in this book too, of course. So, here are some of my favourite examples. Read them, think about them yourself, and I'm sure you can find many more examples from your own experiences of brands and business as well.

I have already introduced some of these cases in other parts of this book. I chose to collect them all here so they can be studied all in one place. In some of these cases I have merely summarized my previous examples and included a reference so you can easily find the full example in a previous chapter. In other cases, I have fleshed them out a little to provide more information and deeper insight.

Some of the examples that follow are well known. In these cases, my comments are shorter and focus mainly on the essence of their surprise and customer experience branding strategy and performance differences.

Other examples may be less well known, or completely new to you. I have chosen these because they are interesting, different and educational. With these cases and businesses, I have allowed more space to explain and ensure they are meaningful and interesting. This doesn't necessarily mean they are better examples, just that they may need a little more storytelling.

Apple: The surprising fruit of user understanding

Apple is one of the most valuable brands on the planet, with the big brand idea of complexity made simple and enjoyable. Every great brand tackles the consumer's enemy and tries to provide a solution to the consumer's problems. Apple takes on the frustration and intimidation that consumers often feel towards technology. The Apple brand promise is to make it easier for us to love technology, to allow everyone to experience the future, no matter who you are.

Apple has expended a lot of effort to create products that take the most complicated technology and deliver it so that anyone can use it. They have done this through a strong sense of user needs and preferences. Apple has been criticized for not being on the leading edge of technology, for copying previously existing technology and calling it unique and new. But being unique and new is not what Apple is about.

This is encapsulated in the famous and often repeated quote from Steve Jobs that sums up what this book is all about: 'You've got to start with the customer experience and work back toward the technology – not the other way around' (Jobs, 1997).

While other geeky IT companies start with the technology and try to force consumers to figure out how to use it, Apple takes that same technology and makes it simpler. Whether it's the iPhone, iPad or Mac, or setting up a Wi-Fi network with Apple AirPort Extreme, Apple makes technology accessible for anyone.

Apple also knows how to tell its stories, starting with its product launches. The launches are covered by the mainstream media and the category press and are talked about in blogs for weeks and months in advance. Apple always shows great self-confidence; they broadcast their launch live online, just like an important top news flash. They have produced very few advertisements over the years, but the ones they have made work well. Apple has learned how to work the media, from CNN to TechCrunch, or any other technology channel, and to social media channels like Twitter and Facebook. Apple has, quite simply, mastered the creation and delivery of a relation brand.

Apple manages the brand experience perfectly. It starts with generating the excitement of anticipated launches and the helpfulness of the Genius Bar and continues with the out-of-box start-up experience of all the Apple products. Yet no matter how much excitement Apple generates, it always seems to over-deliver. You only need to see how giddy people get over their iPhones and iPads. And this contributes towards the love fans have for the Apple brand, and generates a loyal following.

Even when we believe that Apple may be over-dramatizing, we still want to be surprised. And of course, we are. Even if we have monitored the online discussion about what Apple is going to launch next, it is still a surprise. Apple takes full advantage of what I call the Easter egg effect – even though we know almost exactly what is inside, we are still surprised when we take the lid off. In Apple's case, we are surprised because our anticipations are confirmed.

Starbucks: A surprising journey from coffee-freaks to public living rooms

Surprise is doing things in an unpredictable, different way. When the popular impression of fast food emphasises the 'fast', eating on the run in between more important moments, Starbuck does the opposite. You not only feel that it's alright for you to sit with your coffee mug for some time, reading, writing messages on your smartphone or computer, or just having a lengthy conversation with a friend, you're actually encouraged to do it.

According to the story, this insight about how to differentiate Starbucks from similar businesses was unexpected in itself. Starting as a quality coffee provider for discerning coffee aficionados, Starbucks was affected by a supply disaster of labour strikes and low inventory levels in the coffee-growing areas of South America that drove up the price of coffee in 1997 (Schaffler, 1997). Even though Starbucks was unable to deliver the serious, high-quality coffee they promised for a time, in most areas they learned that their customers were not drawn by the quality of the coffee alone. Instead, even with the lower-quality coffee they were temporarily forced to serve, the business went on as usual and Starbucks was one major insight richer. People loved them despite temporarily not getting the high-quality coffee. It was the generous public living room that had become their differentiator in a world of fast-food places, and that was the core of their success

They capitalized on this insight with one of their many campaigns, stressing the value of reading a book. Or rather, stressing the value of having time to read, and think, about anything important while consuming a good cup of coffee. Take your time!

Virgin: Maintaining the predictable and adding the unexpected

Virgin was one of the first typical relation brands, way before its time. When Richard Branson introduced the brand on products from different categories, he was ridiculed by many of the branding specialists of the time. However, Branson was the beacon of the new generation of relation brand builders, and he still is in a more mature phase of relation branding than most others.

From the very beginning, Virgin was a relation brand manifested by Branson personally, but also by its attitude of being revolutionary and entertaining. This was demonstrated at the beginning of airline regulation by its fight with the establishment, symbolized by British Airways (Gregory, 2012), and its foundation in the record business, which was of course entertainment all the way. Ironically, the latter is almost the only business that is not still part of the Virgin empire. Virgin has sought to inspire brands all over the world (Ross, 2016). However, many of them have not understood what it takes to be a relation brand. One of the most important aspects is not to focus on one category of products, but on the brand itself and its relationships, and to drive an issue that is larger than the products. The core of the relationship, and the story of the relation brand, is condensed in the Virgin strategic keywords: revolutionary and entertaining.

Google: A constantly surprising, huge, online creative workshop

It's truly surprising what Google does in every part of life. It is an ongoing, huge experiment and exploration in how to make life on the planet better in every part of our lives.

Google was one of the last search engines to enter the market of internet search tools (Underwood, 2004). Before Google, some very strong brands held the market – Netscape, Yahoo, AltaVista – but from the start, Google handled the search engine market in a surprising way. They offered graded search functions, a search that valued the importance of a webpage and listed pages in order of relevance. Google also offered a way to monetize and commercialize the search in an unexpectedly easy to accept way. It provided, or managed users to perceive, a clear divide between commercial recommendations and the commercially unbiased search results.

The next surprise was that the curiosity of Google's top team was not limited to search engines, but encompassed everything on which the internet had, or could have, an impact. With Google's natural and almost charming self-confidence, consumers were invited to be part of this mission. Whether it is Google Mail, Google Maps or Google Earth, YouTube, Android or Google Glasses, grocery delivery services, medical science projects, space programmes or artificial intelligence programmes, it's hard not to be surprised at what comes out of Google.

Google is a very productive 'human machine' for building a better human life on Earth, including producing profits. Surprise, daring to challenge the unexpected and creating curiosity built the world's strongest (and most valuable) brand, and one of the most successful companies of our time.

Nike: Forever surprisingly fit

Despite having become a large and very experienced company, with proven long-term success, Nike has been the strongest brand of healthy and active lifestyles generation after generation. And it has maintained the ability to surprise us with what it does next. The FuelBand, launched in 2012, was the first in what is now its own category of wearable health devices (Danova, 2015). Surprise has been driving the Nike brand for a long time and will continue to do so.

Lego: Toying with surprising ideas

Lego: The movie is a masterful piece of storytelling, which is surprising to begin with. It is surprising that it makes so much sense to us, and surprising that a Danish toy company can use its brilliant and simple idea to create so much energy, far beyond what is expected from a toy company. To quote the unnamed police officer in the movie: 'You are more than a toy, do you understand?'

It is startling to find that there is a spiritual dimension surprise in pieces of plastic, but Lego is building more than meets the eye. Another surprise is how adults have become one of the company's most important target audiences, with smart technology robotic toys and guns to build, along with special sets for larger buildings. Lego is definitely a surprise brand that is very much aware of its need to surprise the world over and over again.

GoPro: Surprisingly competitive in the smartphone camera world

It is surprising that someone could create a new, billion-dollar camera business when most people already have a high-quality camera in their smartphone. And surprising to see how the company exploited the power of people sharing extreme experiences. (You can read more about GoPro's surprising competitiveness in Chapter 5.)

KLM: A surprisingly generous airline

You don' t expect a mass-transportation company to have an interest in individuals, or to care about finding out what individualized gift it should give in connection with your travel. When KLM did just that, it became more than just an airline. It seemed to be surprisingly interested in me, as a passenger. Or that's what I like to believe. (You can read more about KLM's surprising experiment in Chapter 12.)

Instagram: Surprising insights into sharing photos

A photo is nothing if it is not shared, no matter what filters or technological tricks you may use to make it look better. In building a surprising, easy-to-manage photo album, Instagram continually reminds us how quick and fun it is to share images with friends and family.

In April 2012 Facebook acquired Instagram for one billion dollars (BBC, 2012). Along with Facebook and Twitter, Instagram has become one of the strongest social networks and a very valuable brand-building tool in itself.

H&M: Surprisingly consistent inconsistency

Fashion is characterized by both flocking behaviour and a desire for differentiation (Levy, 2014). Consumers want to belong to a group, while at the same time asserting their individuality, both as a person and through their style.

When H&M sought to define their brand and experience, they chose not to look for or invent something new and different. Instead, they chose to keep it simple and generic. Their business concept is one many retailers can claim: fashion and quality at the best price.

What makes H&M different is that its stores change constantly. H&M decided to build on the constant new supplies and chose to focus on how it did things, rather than what it did. With an ambition to become the 'fun' of fashion, it defined fun by its wide assortment of daily new arrivals, by affordability and unexpected collaborations. These collaborations began with Karl Lagerfeld in 2004. That a fashion retail chain was able to attract famous designers known for their integrity is one of H&M's greatest surprises. And the collaboration with Karl Lagerfeld highlighted its own concept of constant change: Karl embodies the changing nature of fashion. As he has said of himself, 'I never do or say the same thing twice' (Levy, 2014).

Uber: Turning hailing a cab into a surprisingly joyful experience

Uber is changing the transportation industry. It is a successful example to all entrepreneurs who like to use surprise to change the way things that seem unchangeable are experienced. When Uber was introduced, it was an amazing surprise to be able to watch, on your smartphone, how your taxi was approaching. Even return users feel the same surprise and joy, over and over, as they watch their taxi coming closer. And knowing the name of your driver gives you the surprising feeling of control in a situation where you previously had none.

In a business that hasn't changed since it started, Uber's easygoing attitude has been positively surprising, but also intimidating for many traditional taxi companies. The company and its drivers have been threatened, and yet they have held firmly to their mission to change the landscape of the taxi industry.

At the same time, when you reflect about what Uber is actually doing, it is truly surprising how natural and self-evident it feels. Using modern technology and the fact that billions of people carry smartphones, and taking away the middle-man – the taxi firms – to create an international network in more than 300 cities in 50 countries with hundreds of thousands of drivers, mostly with their own cars. Despite negative publicity and allegations of sexual assaults and violence (Linshi, 2014), the game-like feeling of watching your Uber advancing through traffic is an almost addictive, everyday joy.

Handelsbanken: Surprisingly futuristic in finance

Handelsbanken is one of the four big banks in Sweden and Scandinavia. At a time when many customers avoid direct contact with banks, competitors pop up everywhere to challenge banks. Handelsbanken has a different vision of the future, yet in a surprisingly conservative way. As such, Handelsbanken are winning awards alongside the likes of Uber, HBO, Mobileye, Open Garden, Mara Group and Xerox (*Financial Times*, 2015).

Handelsbanken has some of the highest capital ratios and the highest returns in European banking and its business model is conservative with a modern twist. The bank has followed three principles for the past four and a half decades:

1 Customer service transfers into customer satisfaction.
2 Build a bank around what the customer wants.
3 Be thrifty and cost conscious.

When the other major banks set up call centres, Handelsbanken didn't think it would add value for customers, so it did the opposite and gave their customers their personal bank manager's mobile phone number and permission to call at any time. All the customer's dealings with the bank are then through their personal manager. There is no centralized department for support, loan applications or other banking tasks.

The bank's focus on the customer is upheld at all levels of the company. Handelsbanken's chief executive, Pär Boman, periodically spends some time working behind the desk in a local branch, meeting customers and learning what they want (International Banker, 2016).

Handelsbanken also backs a very popular Swedish mobile payment system service called Swish, which is a viable rival to the likes of the e-commerce company Klarna (*Financial Times*, 2015). The bank's approach to modern banking caused analysts at the German investment bank Berenberg to call Handelsbanken 'the blueprint for banking in Europe', and Andy Haldane, Chief Economist at Bank of England, called their business model 'back to the future' (Milne, 2015).

Giffgaff: People-power builds a surprising breakthrough mobile operator brand

At a social media conference in 2009, Guy Thompson, O2's Head of Brand Strategy, was inspired by platforms like Wikipedia and Facebook. He imagined how the new, interactive method those platforms enabled could change everything in the mobile operator market. As a result, Giffgaff was formed: a mobile network run, in part, by its users doing a lot of the work employees would ordinarily handle.

Giffgaff is an independent mobile virtual network operator that runs on the O2 network. From the beginning, its name is a surprise with a double meaning. It's derived from the ancient Scottish term meaning 'mutual giving' (Jamieson, 1808), but the sound of it can also be interpreted as describing a conversation. Taken together, these make the name a perfect description of a social mobile network.

The next big surprise is how Giffgaff encourages its customers to take on the responsibilities of customer services, and rewards them with an internal currency that can be converted into cash, credit or a charitable donation. The goal was to deliver better value, and better and more efficient service than the big networks' call centres.

In this way, O2 created a brand that attracted a sceptical customer group. It was able to create real value for customers, without increasing their costs. Through a focus on simplicity, transparency and rewards, it has developed strong bonds with its customers. And since these loyal customers willingly recruit more, the brand continues to grow, and is branching out into the more mainstream audience. With no call centres or expensive advertising campaigns, the savings could be passed on to consumers, allowing Giffgaff to compete on price in a way that the big networks couldn't.

An altogether surprising strategy and activation of a brand in all the dimensions. Not least on the 'people' axis in the 4-D brand mind space: the social and mental dimensions (see Chapter 6).

Kia Motors: The power of surprise

The power to 'surprise the world by providing exciting and inspiring experiences that go beyond anticipations'. These words from a Kia brochure define the slogan of Kia Motors: 'The Power of Surprise'.

Kia is one of the great surprises of the motoring industry. Its unexpected, future-oriented, smart quality and design surpasses most automotive companies. Its customer-oriented attitude drives the brand's surprise factor.

Kia loves to use the words quality and sustainability to explain its reliability. But what makes it truly surprising, as its brand slogan claims, are the surprises in the customer experience. It presents itself to customers in a surprisingly human, personal and innovative way.

Alibaba Group: Surprisingly passionate

> Money and wealth are two different concepts. If you have money, but have not turned this money into an experience to elevate your own or other people's level of happiness, then you may very well only possess a lot of symbols and a mountain of very colourful pieces of paper.
> Jack Ma, Founder and Chief Executive of Alibaba (CER, 2009)

When Jack Ma founded Alibaba in his kitchen, he had to pool his money together with 17 colleagues because no bank would lend them money. Today, the Alibaba Group is a global leader in e-commerce.

As the tenth anniversary of his company approached in 2005, Jack Ma wrote a letter to his 15,000 employees reflecting on the success of his enterprise. What was the reason for his success – pure luck, or repeatable method? He has explained that the Alibaba Group was built on the following core values:

1 **Customer First.** The first priority of the company is the interests of its users and paying customers.

2 **Teamwork.** Alibaba expects its employees to work as a team. They encourage employee input in making decisions and expect all employees to commit to team objectives.

3 **Embrace change.** The industry Alibaba operates in is evolving rapidly. Consequently, the company asks its employees to be flexible, innovative and to adapt to new conditions and practices.

4 **Integrity.** Trust is an essential element of a marketplace, and Alibaba's employees maintain the highest standards of integrity and deliver on their commitments.

5 **Passion.** Whether serving customers or developing new services and products, Alibaba employees are encouraged to act with passion.

6 **Commitment.** Alibaba has a dedicated focus and commitment to understanding and delivering on the needs of Chinese and global small and medium enterprises.

The company also has a very simple, and strong, mission and vision. Its mission is 'to make it easy to do business anywhere', while the vision has three parts. Alibaba seeks to build a company that will last 102 years, to become the world's largest e-commerce service provider and to become the world's best employer (alibabagroup.com, 2016).

Why 102 years? The company was founded in 1999, which means that 102 years will span three centuries. Jack Ma has chosen to take the long-term view and build lasting sustainability. I also like that the company supports and enables a whole new group of competitors and innovators. With Alibaba's help, enterprises that may not have been able to globally source and sell using the old ways of the corporate west have been able to enter the market. This, in my mind, is truly a brand of the future.

McDonald's, Stockholm: Surprising 'can currency' can purchase hamburgers

In a campaign during the summer of 2015, McDonald's in Sweden surprised Stockholm with a very creative campaign: pay for your burger with cash, cards or recyclable cans.

The price of a Big Mac? Ten cans.

This is a local example of how to be suddenly and temporarily surprising. There is no commitment to honour an offer like this forever. Just the fact that you do it – even if it's only once – is enough. Simply showing that you are a brand that is able to surprise will get you your 'likes'. Any brand, regardless of issue or category, can do that. Just by being a little creative.

Nordic Choice Hotels, Norway (and owner Petter Stordalen): Surprising successful culture from the top

In 2015 *Forbes* magazine named Petter Stordalen, the owner of Nordic Choice Hotels, one of the world's top 'thrillionaires', alongside people like Virgin's Richard Branson and Tesla's Elon Musk (*Forbes*, 2015).

He is a strong, slightly clownish, character who opens his hotels with amazing stunts like landing on the roof of the Clarion Hotel at Arlanda Airport in an electric-blue helicopter and abseiling down the side of the building (Clarion Hotel Arlanda, 2012). In Malmö he arrived James Bond-style on a jet ski, to launch the 400 MUSD Clarion Hotel and Congress Malmö (Ellioth and Winther Film, 2015). In Gothenburg he opened the Clarion Hotel Post by playing drums in a white jumpsuit while being lowered from the roof in a giant disco ball (Clarion Post, 2012).

Stordalen is successful in setting the tone and level of customer experience branding and leaving his people to deliver the details of the experience to customers in a similar style. There is always an element of positive surprise at the hotels in the Nordic Choice Hotel Group's four hotel chains. The 184 hotels in Sweden, Norway, Denmark and the Baltics, with 31,000 rooms, 13,000 employees and 9 million guests in 2015, include licensed brands like Comfort Quality and Quality Resort, Clarion and Clarion Collection, and 10 independent hotels (Nordic Choice Hotels, 2016).

Everywhere, Petter Stordalen has inspired the staff and set the model for customer experience. Despite not being a football fan himself, he uses football fans and their loyalty to their clubs as a benchmark for the loyalty he likes to have within his community of employees.

References

alibabagroup.com (2016) Company overview. [Online] alibabagroup.com [Last accessed: 20.2.16]

BBC (2012) Facebook buys Instagram photo sharing network for $1bn, BBC, 10 April. [Online] www.bbc.com [Last accessed: 23.2.16]

CER (2009) Bad press: Private philanthropy in China has a tarnished public image, but it's all a misunderstanding, *China Economic Review*, 1 December. [Online] www.chinaeconomicreview.com/ [Last accessed: 20.2.16]

Clarion Hotel Arlanda (2012) Petter Stordalen inviger Clarion Hotel Arlanda Airport. [Video, online] vimeo.com/54289593 [Last accessed: 23.2.16]

Clarion Post (2012) Invigningen av Clarion Hotel Post, Göteborg. [Video, online] www.youtube.com/ [Last accessed: 23.2.16]

Danova, T (2015) The entire history of the smartwatch and fitness-band market in one infographic, Business Insider UK, 22 January. [Online] uk.businessinsider.com/ [Last accessed: 23.2.16]

Ellioth and Winther Film (2015) Petter Stordalen: Clarion Hotel & Congress Malmö hotel opening – crashes jet-ski in concrete. [Video, online] vimeo.com/129817968 [Last accessed: 23.2.16]

Financial Times (2015) Handelsbanken winner of *Financial Times* award: Boldness in Business, FT 2015

Forbes (2015) Forbes thrillionaires: With great wealth comes great adventure, 5 January. [Online] www.forbes.com/ [Last accessed: 20.2.16]

Gregory, A (2012) Toxic feud: Just why are Virgin and British Airways always going nose to nose? *Mirror*, 20 April. [Online] mirror.co.uk [Last accessed: 23.1.16]

International Banker (2016) Interview with Pär Boman, CEO of Handelsbanken, *International Banker* 24 February. [Online] internationalbanker.com/ [Last accessed: 23.2.16]

Jamieson, J (1808) *An Etymological Dictionary of the Scottish Language*, University Press, Edinburgh

Jobs, S (1997) 16 brilliant insights from Steve Jobs keynote circa 1997. [Video and transcript, online] onstartups.com/ [Last accessed: 23.2.16]

Levy, M (2014) Uniqlo CMO Jörgen Andersson on Why Consumer Culture is 'generic', Business of Fashion, 1 April. [Online] www.businessoffashion.com/ [Last accessed: 20.2.16]

Linshi, G (2014) Why Uber's rape scandal is more than a 'growing pain', *Time*, 11 December. [Online] time.com/ [Last accessed: 23.2.16]

Milne, R (2015) Handelsbanken is intent on getting banking back to the future, 20 March. [Online] www.ft.com/ [Last accessed: 20.2.16]

Nordic Choice Hotels (2016) State of Nordic Choice Hotels. [Online] http://annualreport.choice.no/en/ [Last accessed: 23.2.16]

Ross, F (2016) The importance of a brand and how to build one. [Online] virgin.com/ [Last accessed: 23.2.16]

Schaffler, R (1997) Coffee is a costly wake-up: Supply shortage has commodity traders bidding up prices, CNN, 6 March. [Online] money.cnn.com/ [Last accessed: 23.2.16]

Underwood, L (2004) A brief history of search engines, Web Reference, 18 August. [Online] www.webreference.com/ [Last accessed: 23.2.16]

Afterword
Putting branding in a larger perspective

In the afterword I want to bring everything together into a bigger picture. It is possible now to look outwards and beyond. Opening philosophically and esoterically can be too great a diversion from the experiences of most business practitioners. At the start, and throughout this book, I have emphasized that branding is a hands-on exercise – much less a strategy and more about tactics, to put it in the military terminology often used in business. At the end of the book I want to emphasize how good business is, in fact, a battle in a large ongoing cosmic war between opposing universal powers.

To set the scene, a powerful video by Ray and Charles Eames, famous Chicago architects through the 1940s to the 1970s, provides us with a visual, emotional experience of where humans fit into the universe (Eames, 1977). I strongly recommend you watch it now; the web address is given in the references list at the end of this afterword.

The video begins at a picnic in Chicago, near the shore of Lake Michigan. From a starting point of one metre square, and one meter above a sleeping man, we take a journey into the outer reaches of the universe, moving 10 times further away and seeing an area 10 times as large every 10 seconds, travelling beyond the atmosphere, past the inner and outer planets of our solar system, out of our own galaxy and past clusters of other galaxies that look like single pinprick stars themselves. From here, we reverse our direction and return to the picnic, and then continue towards the hand of the sleeping man, getting closer by a power of 10 every 10 seconds as we pass layers of skin, into a capillary and a single cell, heading towards a single atomic core in a single carbon molecule and one of the protons that lies within.

What is most striking is that we end up in darkness, emptiness and nothingness in both directions. Whether we look to the outer space or the inner space, darkness, emptiness and nothingness are by far the dominant parts of our entire universe. We humans, our entire physical world and the imaginative world in our minds, represent just a tiny, tiny part of the whole.

Despite our small size in this vast cosmic perspective of nothingness, humans display a lot of self-confidence. In our common view, unless we find life out there that is on a higher level than ourselves, we will perceive ourselves the masters of the universe. We have de facto become masters on our planet, in competition with many versions of aspiring humans who failed to thrive. Our path to success is guided by imagination and culture, produced by a sensational, imaginative intellect that has the ability to see things and live our lives in contexts that are mostly imagined. Therein lies the connection to branding. Yuval Noah Harari's book, *Sapiens: A Brief History of Humankind*, offers further insights into humans and human development, history and, possibly, our future on this planet (Harari, 2015).

My own approach to branding is based on the universal idea of four dimensions (see Chapter 6), with the functional dimension that represents our practical life, the social dimension that represents the connections between all humans, the mental dimension that represents what is important for us individually and the spiritual dimension that represents the bigger issues on our planet.

Within the functional dimension lies our ability to survive and live on this planet. It includes our roles as consumers, users, workers and developers along with the practical handling of details and also bigger issues: threats, including climate and temperature change, sustainability, security and safety, and food and drinkable water. The social dimension is what collectively connects us all together. It is how we communicate and share and promote inclusion. Through the mental dimension we look deeper into the individual. It includes what makes us different, our inner personal vision for our lives. The final spiritual dimension, as I usually point out, is not about religion, but about the bigger picture. It is everything that concerns our collective vision to build a better life on Earth for everyone.

This model is philosophical and archetypal and links back to a much larger perspective: a cultural cosmic scoop that has been important for *Homo sapiens* in its conquest of Earth. A conquest sometimes achieved through light, enlightened, positive forces and positive energies – and sometimes through darker, emptier and more self-destructive forces and energies. Both of these are part of our universe, the outer and inner cosmos.

What's going on in our world, really?

This is our major worry, and yet we are likely to be the only living organism on Earth that is worried about our future. I think the answer to this gigantic question is also the answer to the individual question: why are we never really happy?

We are personally and culturally torn apart by the two opposing major powers of the universe: the dark, empty, self-destructive, doubtful, negative force on one hand and the light, enlightening, progressive, positive force on the other hand. The problem is that the negative forces gain an advantage from the fact that our universe (on both the outer and inner scales) is largely empty, dark, cold and even self-destructive, as evidenced by exploding stars, black holes and the cell death of apoptosis (ALSA, 2016).

The positive forces have not been dormant. On the contrary, they represent the power of being more attractive and positive, full of light, with warmth, life and development. Throughout our history, the dichotomy between light and dark has fuelled all religions and provided a backbone to messages that initially were practical and promoted good social interactions. But history is full of times when the major religions were used by dominant and manipulative people with a darker agenda, bringing periods in which religions became threatening, negative, fearful and evil power tools, justifying major wars and massive destruction.

In our culture as well, predominantly in literature and entertainment, the war-like divide between the positive and negative forces has been a recurring theme. *Star Wars* is just one among the many examples of this story of the two opposing universal forces. The Jedi knights, Obi-Wan Kenobi and Luke Skywalker, represent the positive forces, with the dark Darth Vader clearly representing the negative forces. One of the reasons why *Star Wars* has become such a long-term and enormous entertainment success is that we all literally carry the wars between the two forces within us, and our unconscious minds intuitively identify with the *Star Wars* story.

Branding – set out to support the positive forces in the universe

My definition of branding is 'management of perception in people's minds'. Obviously, this can be misused by people with the wrong intentions, but it can also be used to reinforce the positive, bright, progressive and developing side of our lives. In the connected world we live in today, it means that we have an opportunity to individually share knowledge and identify ourselves with many more people than ever before in our history.

Still, we are only half way there. Facebook has connected more than one billion people (Facebook, 2016), but only 43 per cent of the world's population has regular access to the internet. This leaves 57 per cent, or 4.2 billion people, without regular access, although the fact that more than 80 per cent of the populations of many developed countries are connected online could mean that the whole world will reach this level in the future, or even higher (Broadband Commission for Sustainable Develoment, 2015).

The ideas I have put forward in this book are about how branding can be a positive force in the universe, with a purpose to break through as a source of light and positive energy in the dark, empty, energy-sucking space around us and inside us. In the four dimensions, the spiritual dimension contains a special quest for all brands and their owners: what good are you doing in society, and how does your brand make a positive impact in people's lives?

I believe that branding has both a responsibility to be a positive force and help people to a better life and an opportunity to satisfy people's need for this positive energy. I think this spiritual aspect of what is otherwise materialistic consumption has just begun to become measurable and real in marketing. It will continue as we become more mature in this connected world and will play a much greater part in the choices we make of products, services, places to visit and experiences. We will demand positive energies from brands more than we will expect them to deliver functionally. This idea of a psychological bonding between people and brands – relation brands – began when Susan Fournier published her scientific paper Consumers and their brands: Developing relationship theory in consumer research (Fournier, 1998), and it has continued ever since.

Brands and companies, and nations and regions, across the world have been able to show how one can do good for people and the environment while maintaining a positive growth and a healthy business. The ability to do both what is good for your company and what is good for mankind is not seen as impossible today. We have evidence that it works in Scandinavia, and in Sweden in particular. Sweden has successfully combined fewer emissions with a better economy (Sweden.se, 2016).

Sweden also has many examples of brands and companies that are growing and doing well while still taking greater responsibility for sustainability, including causing fewer emissions than many of their competitors. Examples of international Swedish companies that have incorporated this mind-set are H&M and IKEA. H&M has dedicated itself both to sustainability, through sustainable resources and better working conditions, and to driving positive change that lasts through the H&M Conscious Foundation (H&M, 2016). IKEA's move towards sustainability includes goals of 100 per cent renewable energy and sustainable sourcing in a drive for 'Resource and energy independence', along with building 'A better life for people and communities' (IKEA, 2015).

All this increases the bonds between people, and brands can act as facilitators of this bonding by sharing experiences and interest. Brands will bring us together, creating intermediate relationship links and helping us to identify with and empathize with our fellow human beings on an intensely individual basis. That should lead to a better world.

I hope that everyone who reads and studies this book will find the part they alone can play in this positive future.

References

ALSA (2016) Cell death and apoptosis, ALS Association. [Online] www.alsa.org [Last accessed: 26.2.16]

Broadband Commission for Sustainable Development (2015) *The State of Broadband 2015: Broadband as a foundation for sustainable development.* [Online] broadbandcommission.org/publications/ [Last accessed: 26.2.16]

Eames, C and Eames, R (1977) Powers of ten. [Video, online] https://youtu.be/ 5CKd0aPSWe8 [Last accessed: 26.2.16]

Facebook (2016) Company information. [Online] http://newsroom.fb.com/ company-info/ [Last accessed: 26.2.16]

H&M (2016) About H&M. [Online] about.hm.com/ [Last accessed: 26.2.16]

Harari, YN (2015) *Sapiens: A brief history of humankind*, Harper Collins, New York

IKEA (2015) *2015 Sustainability Report*, Ikea. [Online] www.ikea.com/ms/en_US/ this-is-ikea/people-and-planet/ [Last accessed: 26.2.16]

Fournier, S (1998) Consumers and their brands: Developing relationship theory in consumer research, *Journal of Customer Research*, **24**, pp 343–373 (March)

Sweden.se (2016) Sweden tackles climate change, Sweden Sverige. [Online] sweden.se/nature/sweden-tackles-climate-change/ [Last accessed: 26.2.16]

Notes

Transaction brands as opposed to relation brands

Transaction brands and relation brands make up the backbone of my view on branding. To understand the dramatic difference between these two types of brands, this section provides details on transaction brands as opposed to relation brands, thereby clarifying what relation brands are not. This section also outlines the background and historical context of transaction brands: their drivers and characteristics in marketing, selling, communication, innovation and behaviour.

The world of transaction brands

With industrialism, everything changed. The introduction of mass production changed more than the social lives of workers, national economics or politics. Most of all, industrialism changed the lives of consumers. A world of more or less individualised craftsmanship changed into a world of serial production and economies of scale. Most of what we consume and use every day was made possible only through the means of mass production.

At the same time, the mass production of industrialism also taught us consumers the new rule of the industrial era: acceptance. Acceptance of the conformity of products (or services) required by production that follows economy of scale. Henry Ford's famous quote about his model T-Ford signifies the change of mind-set that was needed: 'You can have it in any colour you like, as long as it's black'.

Now, of course, the industry offers plenty of choice, not only in the colour of a car, but also with advanced personalisation (such as with the VW Individual) with hundreds of equipment and style options to choose from. This plethora of options is found everywhere, even with toothpaste (such as Colgate) that offers many different flavours and active ingredients for different types of dental condition. But these offerings of choice are still driven by industry, and offered on the producers' own terms.

Mass production needed transaction brands

Mass production also created new problems. Initially, overproduction was tempting, because the price could be reduced with a longer series. A new and different system of mass distribution was created that included regional storage and warehouses along with freight consolidators and distributers, supermarkets, discount retailers, and so on. And mass marketing was created in order to drive the sales through the whole of the distribution chain.

This mass marketing essentially pushed products, and later packaged services as well, to the consumer. A new type of brand was created as a vehicle for this mass marketing. This is what I now prefer to call the transaction brand promoted by mass communication. All of this followed the economy of scale idea from factory to consumer. The messages were simplified and repeated mechanically. Just as the production was mechanised, so was the advertising.

In effect, the consumer was brainwashed with simple brand-messages from these transaction brands. The mass media that transmitted this brainwashing proved to be highly successful; investing one dollar gave three dollars or more in increased business.

Mass marketing not only solved the problem of overproduction, it actually created a consumer demand and a need for increased production. And everyone along the distribution chain reaped the benefits. Huge businesses like Proctor & Gamble, Unilever and Nestle, were built on the foundations of these powerful new investment mechanisms. Mass marketing developed new tools to research and measure consumers, and invented complex segmentation models, based on socio-demographics, to target, predict and control the influence of consumer attitudes, patterns and preferences.

And these investments in branding, mass marketing, mass communication and advertising to consumers became one of the biggest businesses of our time. The transaction brands spent billions of dollars on brainwashing, mainly using TV advertising. This, in turn, helped establish TV as the leading medium, although other mass media also benefited from the wave of transaction brand building. The rest, as they say, is history... although it is still going on, just perhaps not with the same strength as before. In 2008, internet advertising overtook TV advertising as the leading media in many Western countries, in terms of money spent.

While the development of most transaction brands took 20 to 40 years, relation brands have sped up the process to reach the same level of brand equity in just 5 to 15 years. This is the obvious reason why many businesses now choose relation branding over transaction branding; it is quicker and cheaper. Because the relation brand is not built by advertising, there is less need for upfront cash. Instead, relation brands are built through internet activities, social events, co-branding and word-of-mouth from proud users who interact through blogs and who form an active brand community. These and other social activities are not simply channels of communication similar to old-school media; they are integral parts of the brand and, of course, supporting it.

Both of these types of brand will continue to co-exist, probably forever. Even though relation brands come from the new school, neither is inherently better. In fact, in evaluations by classical transaction brand consultants, such as Interbrand's brand value evaluation published annually in *Business Week*, we see transaction and relation brands standing shoulder to shoulder in terms of monetary value. This is especially interesting, since relation brands have not made major investments in advertising. Any investments they have made are just a fraction of the investments usually made by transaction brands.

They both have their advantages and disadvantages, and neither of the two is coming out as the only survivor. As a brand builder, you have to make the choice of which way to go. The answer is usually how much you are willing to change your company; how much you are willing to embrace relation branding as your company culture. This, of course, depends on the attitudes and personalities in the management team, and may also depend on the traditions inherent in different businesses.

Transaction brand characteristics

The first typical characteristic of a transaction brand is its extreme focus on the product or service. The brand becomes what is usually called a trust-mark for product quality, performance, design and usage. This is an absolutely natural thing for a transaction brand; the whole idea is to promote one product or one service. The failure of a new product is serious for a transaction brand. If the product is wrong it will bring the whole brand down. That's why a transaction branded product has to be tested multiple times in product trials, focus groups, and torture-tests before it is finally launched. A few examples of transaction brands are: Coca-Cola, Ford, McDonalds, Marlboro, BMW.

For transaction brands generally, all the brand equity – the value of the brand – is tied to the products. If the product fails, the brand fails. Therefore, it is usually of utmost importance never to deviate from the lines of the transaction brand script. That is why transaction brands have very, very detailed brand manuals. They are so detailed that the transaction brands can recruit any young graduate from any business school to become their brand manager. This used to surprise me when I worked for some of these transaction brand companies, until I realised that literally everything in the execution of brand communication, innovation, and behaviour was typically regulated in detail in their comprehensive brand books. This, too, is logical, since the brand is the product and the product the brand.

The logic of the transaction brand was that it's not the company behind the product, but the product itself that is interesting to the consumer. Thus one of the favourite words for transaction brand is *relevance*. For the consumer.

Proctor & Gamble is a good example of a company that has very successfully built a relation brand out of its corporate brand. They very cleverly used social media, mainly on Facebook, for its 'mother' campaigns, with themes like 'Mother always knows best' and 'Mothers' Day', that have celebrated the mother, who is traditionally responsible for household purchases. It has even tried to humanise its product brands, like Fairy, but it remains constrained by the culture of their product branding.

Another example of this is Ford. While the focus is still very much on the products, Ford has built more of the company brand into its product brands, as with the Ford Mondeo.

Selling transaction brands

We have already discussed how the marketing of transaction brands grew from industrialism, and created its own industry: the mass marketing and mass communication media world. We now turn to the selling: how are the transaction brands sold by their salesmen? If the marketing was inspired by industrialism, the selling is inspired by politics.

I usually find the typical transaction brand salesman is very similar to a politician: product politicians who put themselves on a real or virtual podium and literally speak down to the audience. In fact, *audience* is the term usually used by transaction brand marketers. They try to convince us, the less-initiated or knowledgeable common people, of the advantages of choosing their products or services. Unfortunately, every so often this comes with an arrogant 'from above' attitude that arises from (self-) confidence in your own product along with the distance to the audience. And this is a serious and very important mistake in today's world. It is a lack of respect, 'delivering messages to undifferentiated hordes who didn't want to receive them,' as Doc Searls and David Weinberger express it in their excellent documentation of the new importance of conversing with individuals rather than giving speeches to audiences, *The Cluetrain Manifesto* (Levine *et al*, 2001).

For true transaction brand builders this probably sounds like a lot of nonsense. They probably would ask: 'How can you sell if you're not confident, pushing your arguments, creating respect?' If that is the case, it's typical and sad. We see a huge gap in attitudes between the two types of brands. And this is exactly why it's so difficult to switch from being a transaction brand to being a relation brand.

Innovation in a transaction brand

Innovation is particularly tricky for a transaction brand with so much focus on one product (or service). Remember, the brand is the product and the product is the brand, and some of these transaction branded products have become highly profiled and specific.

Let's take the well-known example of Coca-Cola. The slightest change in the product will provoke consumers; when Coca-Cola changed the taste some time ago the consumers protested – 'this is not how Coke is supposed to taste'. The new taste was rejected and Coca-Cola had to return to the classic taste (Brown, 2012). Any new product will be difficult for Coca-Cola, any innovation under that name questionable, but still Coca-Cola works on innovations, and that is the most amazing part. When you have the perfect product so tightly linked to a certain brand, why try to challenge that with innovations?

But transaction brands in similar situation usually do. The answer must be a slightly paranoid: 'If we don't try all the time, someone else may try to challenge us.' This innovation urge doesn't become easier if you, as a transaction brand, are so focused on your product and thus very demanding when it comes to the kind of innovation that's expected. It usually has to be the new *big* idea. Anything less is uninteresting. And since the product is the brand to such a degree, the innovation work has to be done with the greatest secrecy. Developed in closed laboratories, tested on focus groups under the severest non-disclosure agreements, and then finally launched, synchronised, on all shelves, in every corner of the world at the same time.

You may feel I exaggerate, and maybe I do, but my point is that the innovation work for a transaction brand is filled with trauma. Despite having large research and development departments, the new ideas generated are seldom good enough to replace, or even complement, the hero product of the brand. What typical transaction brands do is take their best new ideas or acquisitions and simply put them under a new transaction brand, rather than try to squeeze them in under the existing brand and risk destroying it.

When McDonald's was criticised for promoting obesity, they had to put a lot of research and development power into developing new, healthier food on their menus. But the fact that the brand is so intimately connected with the Big Mac hamburger (perceived as not healthy) means that these new, healthier product innovations will have a hard time changing the brand's positioning. Still, McDonald's is a brand loved by the people who love hamburgers... and that is more than fine for a brand!

Can a transaction brand become a relation brand?

I frequently get asked this question, and my answer is: theoretically it should be possible, but in reality it's much more difficult. The differences in management attitude, corporate culture and belief systems are huge between these two types of brand cultures. This makes it hard to switch from one to the other. In a personal conversation with top Coca-Cola executives, I learned that Coca-Cola is flirting with the idea of relation brands and trying to personalise their products by putting people's names on the Coke cans. It's interesting to note that Coca-Cola is also running very large, ambitious and quite successful social media programmes. It even shares videos on the internet in which the company explains how it manages its social media marketing and public relations approaches. Most transaction brands are aware of the situation and are flirting with the idea of relation branding in a similar way, with no illusions that it will work completely (Brown, 2012).

Examples of transaction brands include Coca-Cola, Ford, McDonald's, Marlboro and BMW.

References

Brown, A (2012) How we built Coca-Cola Journey, Unbottled [Blog, online] http://www.coca-colacompany.com/coca-cola-unbottled/how-we-built-coca-cola-journey/ [Last accessed: 25.1.16]

Levine, F, Locke, C, Searls, D and Wineberger, D (2001) *The Cluetrain Manifesto*, Basic Books, Cambridge, MA

McCracken, G (2005) *Culture and Consumption II: Markets, Meaning and Brand Management*, Indiana University Press, Bloomington

INDEX

Italics indicate a figure or table.